READY-TO-USE READING BINGOS, PUZZLES, AND RESEARCH ACTIVITIES FOR THE ELEMENTARY SCHOOL YEAR

Barbara Farley Bannister

THE CENTER FOR APPLIED RESEARCH IN EDUCATION
West Nyack, New York 10995

© 1989 by
THE CENTER FOR APPLIED
RESEARCH IN EDUCATION
West Nyack, New York 10995

All rights reserved

Permission is given for individual librarians and classroom teachers to reproduce the game, puzzle, and student activity pages for classroom and library use. Reproduction of these materials for an entire school system is strictly forbidden.

1 2 3 4 5 6 7 8 9 10

Library of Congress Cataloging-in Publication Data

Bannister, Barbara Farley.
   Ready-to-use reading bingos, puzzles, and research activities for the elementary school year / Barbara Farley Bannister.
     p. cm.
   ISBN 0-87628-787-9
   1. Reading games. 2. Reading (Elementary) I. Center for Applied Research in Education. II. Title.
LB1050.4.B36 1989
372.4′14—dc20   89-37256
                                                                             CIP

ISBN 0-87628-787-9

**THE CENTER FOR APPLIED
RESEARCH IN EDUCATION**
BUSINESS & PROFESSIONAL DIVISION
A division of Simon & Schuster
West Nyack, New York 10995

Printed in the United States of America

DEDICATION: With love to my parents

ACKNOWLEDGEMENTS

Thanks to Christine Allen for introducing me to the idea of Reading Bingos and to Stan Hushbeck of QUAILRIDGE MEDIA for allowing me to write and include in this book new Student Detective and Crossword Count activities.

ABOUT THE AUTHOR

Barbara Farley Bannister attended the University of Nebraska and graduated from Western Michigan University in Kalamazoo. She has taught library skills on all grade levels from K–6 and reading enrichment to students in grades 3–6 and is currently a librarian/teacher at Memorial Elementary School in McMinnville, Oregon.

Mrs. Bannister is the author of two other books for elementary librarians and teachers, *Library Media Center Activities for Every Month of the School Year* (1986) and *Reading Round-Ups: 130 Ready-to-Use Literature Enrichment Activities for Grades 5–8* (1988), both published by The Center for Applied Research in Education. She is an active member of the Oregon Educational Media Association and the National Education Association.

About This Resource

Ready-to-Use Reading Bingos, Puzzles and Research Activities for the Elementary School Year is designed to give busy librarians and classroom teachers a store of ready-to-use material to stimulate student reading and research from September through June. For easy use the book is organized into three main units, one for each season of the school year. The game components, activity sheets, and student awards included can be reproduced just as they appear, as many times as you need them, for use with individual students, small groups, or an entire class.

Each seasonal section begins with several Reading Bingos for use during that season to encourage students to read a variety of fiction and nonfiction books. Next, it presents two Student Detective Research Activities and two or three Crossword Count Dictionary Puzzles that focus on the use of basic research tools to locate specific information. These are followed by a number of Research Activities appropriate to the season designed to provide further practice in the use of reference books and library resources. All of this material is accompanied by easy-to-follow teacher directions for effective use, answer keys where appropriate, and reproducible achievement awards.

The Reading Bingos are adaptable to either classroom or library and can be used with any age group able to read the related books. All students can participate at their own reading level and can read the five books necessary to win. While it is best to use only two or three of the bingos during one school year, more have been included here to give the teacher or librarian a variety from year to year and the opportunity to select one that best fits their need.

For example, Unit I includes SHARE A SCARE READING BINGO, which features "scary" or mystery books, and OUR AMERICAN HERITAGE READING BINGO, which features nonfiction and historical fiction books about the United States. This section also includes OUR CANADIAN HERITAGE READING BINGO for students in Canada, or students in the United States who are studying about our great neighbor to the north.

Each unit's Student Detective Research Activities emphasize research in many areas of the reference section and also encourage students to think about the different reference sources that might be needed. "The Student Detective and the Case of the Mystery Winter Vacation," for example, calls for research in an atlas.

Some of these activities are suitable for gifted groups since they encourage higher-level thinking skills. However, most of the activities are appropriate for all students when the teacher provides help with the directions and the choice of reference sources.

The Crossword Count Puzzles, with a seasonal theme included in each unit, encourage students to use the dictionary to find words with letters having a high point count so that they can achieve the highest score for their grade level. These are suitable as class activities and also as contests in the library or classroom.

The many Research Activities at the end of each unit relate to special days and events of the season. Autumn's unit, for example, includes an activity for National Children's Book Week as well as activities for Veteran's Day, Halloween, and Thanksgiving. The winter section includes activities for Christmas, New Year's, the Chinese Zodiac, and other special days, such as Valentine's Day and St. Patrick's Day. Also included are interesting activities which could be used while teaching a unit on fairytales. Spring activities include one each for Mother's Day, Father's Day, and National Library Week, and others which feature spring or summer events.

A special "Skills Index" is provided after the Table of Contents to help you easily locate activities appropriate to what you are teaching. Many activities, such as the Reading Bingos and Crossword Count Puzzles, are suitable for use with students at all grade and ability levels. Others are best suited to specific grade levels, and this is so indicated in the "Skills Index" as well as on the teacher directions page accompanying each activity. Most of the teacher pages also include space where you can write notes concerning your use of the activity or ideas you have used to enhance it.

Librarians, teachers, and students will all find that they enjoy doing the activities in this book.

Barbara Farley Bannister

CONTENTS

About This Resource v

Skills Index xiii

Unit I. AUTUMN ACTIVITIES 1

    A. AUTUMN READING BINGOS
        Directions for Reading Bingos (5)
        Directions for Autumn Reading Bingos (6)

        SHARE A SCARE READING BINGO
            Student Bingo Card (8)
            Bulletin Board Squares (9)
            Bookmarks and Notes from Home (14)
            Certificates (15)

        OUR AMERICAN HERITAGE READING BINGO
            Student Bingo Card (16)
            Bulletin Board Squares (17)
            Bookmarks and Notes from Home (22)
            Certificates (23)

        OUR CANADIAN HERITAGE READING BINGO
            Student Bingo Card (24)
            Bulletin Board Squares (25)
            Bookmarks and Notes from Home (30)
            Certificates (31)

    B. AUTUMN STUDENT DETECTIVE ACTIVITIES
        Directions for Use of Student Detective Activities (32)

        THE STUDENT DETECTIVE AND THE CASE OF THE MISSING FOOTBALL
            Teacher Directions and Key (33)

Student Activity Page (34)
Certificates (35)

THE STUDENT DETECTIVE AND THE CASE OF THE MISSING MARCHING BAND
Teacher Directions and Key (36)
Student Activity Page (37)
Certificate (38)

C. AUTUMN CROSSWORD COUNT PUZZLES
Directions for Using Crossword Count Puzzles (39)
Record of Scores for Autumn Crossword Count Puzzles (40)

BACK TO SCHOOL CROSSWORD COUNT
Student Activity Page (41)
Certificates (42)

A PILGRIM THANKSGIVING CROSSWORD COUNT
Student Activity Page (43)
Certificates (44)

D. RESEARCH ACTIVITIES FOR AUTUMN

RESEARCH BINGO FOR AUTUMN
Teacher Directions and Key (45)
Student Activity Page (46)

THE COLORS OF AUTUMN
Teacher Directions and Key (47)
Student Activity Page (48)

IT HAPPENED IN THE AUTUMN
Teacher Directions and Key (49)
Student Activity Page (50)

IN AUTUMN IT'S APPLE TIME!
Teacher Directions and Key (51)
Student Activity Page (52)

ENCYCLOPEDIA RESEARCH ACTIVITIES FOR HALLOWEEN
Teacher Directions and Key (53)
Student Activity Pages (54)

BEAT THE WITCH TO THE PUMPKIN PATCH I & II
Teacher Directions and Keys (60)
Student Activity Page for I (61)
Student Activity Page for II (62)

HALLOWEEN FUN WITH THE DICTIONARY
Teacher Directions and Key (63)
Student Activity Page (64)

A PUZZLE FOR VETERAN'S DAY
Teacher Directions and Key (65)
Student Activity Page (66)

Contents

WHO IS THIS CHARACTER? A NATIONAL CHILDREN'S BOOK WEEK ACTIVITY
Teacher Directions and Key (67)
Sample Poster (68)
Student Activity Page (69)

THAT'S THE PERFECT BOOK FOR YOU
Teacher Directions and Key (70)
Student Activity Page (71)

THANKSGIVING ART AND RESEARCH
Teacher Directions and Key (72)
Student Activity Page (73)

UNIT II. WINTER ACTIVITIES 75

A. WINTER READING BINGOS
Directions for Winter Reading Bingos (79)

ONCE-UPON-A-TIME READING BINGO
Teacher Directions (79)
Student Bingo Card (81)
Bulletin Board Squares (82)
Bookmarks and Notes from Home (87)
Certificates (88)

FAVORITE AUTHORS READING BINGO
Teacher Directions (89)
Student Bingo Card (91)
Bulletin Board Squares (92)
Student Bingo Card (Primary) (94)
Bulletin Board Squares (96)
Bookmarks and Notes from Home (98)
Certificates (99)

B. WINTER STUDENT DETECTIVE ACTIVITIES

THE STUDENT DETECTIVE WINS A HOLIDAY BIKE
Teacher Directions and Key (100)
Student Activity Page (102)
Certificates (103)

THE STUDENT DETECTIVE AND THE CASE OF THE MYSTERY WINTER VACATION
Teacher Directions and Key (104)
Student Activity Page (105)
Certificates (106)

C. WINTER CROSSWORD COUNT PUZZLES
Directions for Winter Crossword Count Puzzles (107)
Record of Scores for Winter Crossword Count Puzzles (108)

FUN IN THE SNOW CROSSWORD COUNT
   Student Activity Page (109)
   Certificates (110)
CUPID—A VALENTINE CROSSWORD COUNT
   Student Activity Page (111)
   Certificates (112)
LUCK OF THE IRISH CROSSWORD COUNT
   Student Activity Page (113)
   Certificates (115)

D. FUN WITH FAIRYTALES
   Teacher Directions and Suggestions (116)
WANTED...
   Teacher Directions and Key (117)
   Student Activity Page (118)
FAIRYTALE ELEMENTS FOR CREATIVE WRITING
   Teacher Directions (119)
   Reproducible Page (120)
   Creative Writing Student Page (121)
A MYSTERY MESSAGE FOR FAIRYTALE EXPERTS
   Teacher Directions and Key (122)
   Student Activity Page (123)
FAIRYTALE ACTIVITIES
   Teacher Activities (124)
   Student Activity Page (125)

E. RESEARCH ACTIVITIES FOR WINTER

A HOLIDAY BOOK SCRAMBLE
   Teacher Directions and Key (126)
   Student Activity Page (127)
HOLIDAY RESEARCH A & B
   Teacher Directions and Keys (128)
   Student Page for HOLIDAY RESEARCH A (129)
   Student Page for HOLIDAY RESEARCH B (130)
WHO SAID IT?
   Teacher Directions and Key (131)
   Student Activity Page (132)
DECEMBER DICTIONARY FUN
   Teacher Directions and Key (133)
   Student Activity Page (134)
HAPPY NEW YEAR
   Teacher Directions and Key (135)
   Student Activity Page (136)
THE CHINESE ZODIAC
   Teacher Directions and Key (137)

Student Activity Page (138)
VALENTINES FOR FAMOUS PEOPLE
   Teacher Directions and Key (139)
   Student Activity Page (140)
GREEN IS FOR THE IRISH
   Teacher Directions (141)
   Shamrocks for Card Catalog Usage (143)
   Blank Shamrock Page for Individual Collections (145)
A ST. PATRICK'S DAY JOURNEY
   Teacher Directions (146)
   Student Activity Page (147)
HELP THE LEPRECHAUN FIND THE POT OF GOLD
   Teacher Directions and Key (148)
   Student Activity Page (149)

UNIT III. SPRING ACTIVITIES 151

A. SPRING READING BINGOS
      Directions for Spring Reading Bingos (155)
   I LOVE BOOKS READING BINGO
      Teacher Directions (155)
      Student Bingo Card (157)
      Bulletin Board Squares (158)
      Bookmarks and Notes from Home (163)
      Certificate (164)
   LET'S TRAVEL READING BINGO
      Teacher Directions (165)
      Student Bingo Card (166)
      Bulletin Board Squares (167)
      Bookmarks and Notes from Home (172)
      Certificate (173)

B. ANIMAL READING PROGRAM FOR THE PRIMARY GRADES
      Teacher Directions (174)
      Student Record Sheet (176)
      Animal Record Patterns (177)
      Student Notes for Home (179)
      Certificates (180)

C. SPRING STUDENT DETECTIVE ACTIVITIES
   THE STUDENT DETECTIVE AND THE CASE OF THE APRIL FOOL JOKER
      Teacher Directions and Key (181)
      Student Activity Page (182)
      Certificates (183)

THE STUDENT DETECTIVE AND THE CASE OF THE MYSTERY
INVITATION
    Teacher Directions and Key (184)
    Student Activity Page (185)
    Certificates (186)

D. SPRING CROSSWORD COUNT PUZZLES
    Directions and Record of Scores for Spring Crossword Count Puzzles (187)

   WELCOME SPRING CROSSWORD COUNT
       Student Activity Page (189)
       Certificates (190)
   A BUSY TIME FOR BEES! CROSSWORD COUNT
       Student Activity Page (191)
       Certificates (192)

E. RESEARCH ACTIVITIES FOR SPRING

   SPRINGTIME IS BIRD TIME
       Teacher Directions and Key (193)
       Student Activity Page (194)
   HELP THE BUNNY FIND HIS BASKET!
       Teacher Directions and Key (195)
       Student Activity Page (196)
   DICTIONARY FUN FOR MOTHER'S DAY
       Teacher Directions and Key (197)
       Student Activity Page (198)
   IT HAPPENED IN THE SPRINGTIME
       Teacher Directions and Key (199)
       Student Activity Page (200)
   A SUMMER VACATION IN CANADA
       Teacher Directions and Key (201)
       Student Activity Page (202)
   HIP, HIP, HOORAY FOR FATHER'S DAY
       Teacher Directions and Key (203)
       Student Activity Page (204)
   THROUGH THE SUMMERTIME
       Teacher Directions and Key (205)
       Student Activity Page (206)

SKILLS INDEX

SKILL	PAGE	GRADE LEVELS
READING APPRECIATION		
Autumn Reading Bingos	5	All Reading Levels
Who Is This Character?	67	K–6
That's the Perfect Book for You	70	4–6
Winter Reading Bingos	79	All Reading Levels
Fun with Fairytales	116	3–5
Holiday Book Scramble	126	3–5
Spring Reading Bingos	155	All Reading Levels
Animal Reading Program for the Primary Grades	174	K–3
RESEARCH IN THE DICTIONARY		
Back-to-School Crossword Count	41	All Reading Levels
A Pilgrim Thanksgiving Crossword Count	43	All Reading Levels
Halloween Fun with the Dictionary	63	2–4
Thanksgiving Art and Research	72	2–4
Fun in the Snow Crossword Count	109	All Reading Levels
Cupid, a Valentine Crossword Count	111	All Reading Levels
Luck of the Irish Crossword Count	113	All Reading Levels
December Dictionary Fun	133	2–4
Dictionary Fun for Mother's Day	197	2–4
RESEARCH IN THE ENCYCLOPEDIA		
Encyclopedia Research Activities for Halloween	53	3–4
The Chinese Zodiac	137	3–6

SKILL	PAGE	GRADE LEVELS
RESEARCH IN THE ALMANAC		
Happy New Year	135	4–8
It Happened in the Springtime	199	4–8
RESEARCH IN ATLAS		
The Student Detective and the Case of the Mystery Winter Vacation	104	5–8
RESEARCH IN THE CARD CATALOG		
The Colors of Autumn	47	3–5
RESEARCH WITH DEWEY DECIMAL		
A St. Patrick's Day Journey	146	4–8
RESEARCH IN BOOK OF QUOTATIONS		
Who Said It?	131	5–8
RESEARCH WITH MORE THAN ONE SOURCE		
Student Detective and the Case of the Missing Football (Almanac and Encyclopedia)	33	4–6
Student Detective and the Case of the Missing Marching Band (Almanac, Encyclopedia, Dictionary)	36	4–6
Research Bingo for Autumn (Card Catalog, Almanac, Dictionary, Encyclopedia, Thesaurus)	45	5–8
It Happened in the Autumn (Card Catalog, Encyclopedia, Almanac)	49	5–8
In Autumn It's Apple Time! (Almanac Dictionary, Book of Quotations, *Guinness Book of World Records*, *Famous First Facts*, Encyclopedia)	51	6–8
A Puzzle for Veteran's Day (Encyclopedia, Almanac)	65	4–6
Student Detective Wins a Holiday Bike (Almanac, Card Catalog, Book of Quotations, Encyclopedia)	100	5–8

Skills Index

SKILL	PAGE	GRADE LEVELS
Holiday Research A (Card Catalog and Dictionary)	128	3–4
Holiday Research B (Book of Quotations, Card Catalog, *Guinness Book of World Records*, *Famous First Facts*, Encyclopedia)	128	5–8
Valentines for Famous People (Almanac, Card Catalog, Encyclopedia)	139	4–6
Help the Leprechaun Find the Pot of Gold (Almanac and Encyclopedia)	148	4–6
Student Detective and the Case of the April Fool Joker (*Famous First Facts*, Almanac, Encyclopedia, *Guinness Book of World Records*)	181	4–8
Student Detective and the Case of the Mystery Invitation (Almanac, Dictionary, Encyclopedia)	184	5–8
Springtime Is Bird Time (Almanac, Card Catalog)	193	4–6
Help the Bunny Find His Basket (Almanac, Dictionary)	195	4–8
A Summer Vacation in Canada (Encyclopedia, Almanac)	201	4–8
Hip, Hip, Hooray for Father's Day (Dewey Decimal, Card Catalog)	203	4–6
Through the Summertime	205	4–6

UNIT I
Autumn Activities

Activity

A. AUTUMN READING BINGOS
   Directions for Reading Bingos
   Directions for Autumn Reading
     Bingos

   SHARE A SCARE READING
     BINGO
   Student Bingo Card
   Bulletin Board Squares
   Bookmarks and Notes from Home
   Certificates

   OUR AMERICAN HERITAGE
     READING BINGO
   Student Bingo Card
   Bulletin Board Squares
   Bookmarks and Notes from Home
   Certificates

   OUR CANADIAN HERITAGE
     READING BINGO
   Student Bingo Card
   Bulletin Board Squares
   Bookmarks and Notes from Home
   Certificates

Skills Used

Reading Appreciation

Activity	*Skills Used*
B. AUTUMN STUDENT DETECTIVE ACTIVITIES Directions for Use of Student Detective Activities	Research
THE STUDENT DETECTIVE AND THE CASE OF THE MISSING FOOTBALL Teacher Directions and Key Student Activity Page Certificates	Almanac, Encyclopedia
THE STUDENT DETECTIVE AND THE CASE OF THE MISSING MARCHING BAND Teacher Directions and Key Student Activity Page Certificates	Almanac, Encyclopedia, Dictionary
C. AUTUMN CROSSWORD COUNT PUZZLES Directions for Using Crossword Count Puzzles Record of Scores for Autumn Crossword Count Puzzles	
BACK TO SCHOOL CROSSWORD COUNT Student Activity Page Certificates	Dictionary
A PILGRIM THANKSGIVING CROSSWORD COUNT Student Activity Page Certificates	Dictionary
D. RESEARCH ACTIVITIES FOR AUTUMN	
RESEARCH BINGO FOR AUTUMN Teacher Directions and Key Student Activity Page	Card Catalog, Almanac, Dictionary, Encyclopedia, Shelving, Thesaurus
THE COLORS OF AUTUMN Teacher Directions and Key Student Activity Pages	Card Catalog, Shelving

Autumn Activities

Activity *Skills Used*

IT HAPPENED IN THE AUTUMN
Teacher Directions and Key
Student Activity Page

Thinking Skills, Card Catalog, Encyclopedia, Almanac

IN AUTUMN IT'S APPLE TIME!
Teacher Directions and Key
Student Activity Page

Book of Quotations, *Guinness Book of Records*, Almanac, Encyclopedia, Dictionary, *Famous First Facts*

ENCYCLOPEDIA ACTIVITIES
FOR HALLOWEEN
Teacher Directions and Key
Student Activity Page

Encyclopedia

CAN YOU BEAT THE WITCH TO
THE PUMPKIN PATCH?
Teacher Directions and Keys
Student Activity Pages for I and II

Dictionary, Card Catalog, Encyclopedia, Almanac

HALLOWEEN FUN WITH THE
DICTIONARY
Teacher Directions and Key
Student Activity Page

Dictionary

A PUZZLE FOR VETERAN'S DAY
Teacher Directions and Key
Student Activity Page

Encyclopedia, Almanac

WHO IS THIS CHARACTER? A
NATIONAL BOOK WEEK
ACTIVITY
Teacher Directions
Sample Completed Activity Page
Student Activity Page

Reading Appreciation

THAT'S THE PERFECT BOOK
FOR YOU
Teacher Directions and Key
Student Activity Page

Reading Appreciation, Thinking Skills

THANKSGIVING ART AND
RESEARCH
Teacher Directions and Key
Student Activity Page

Dictionary

A. Autumn Reading Bingos

DIRECTIONS FOR READING BINGOS

Reading Bingos may be used in either a classroom or the media center. They are intended to not only encourage children to read but also encourage them to expand the scope of their reading since there are five different books, usually of a different type which they must read in order to bingo. While hoping to encourage the less enthusiastic reader since everyone who reads five in a row may win, it also usually stimulates the good readers who often try to get several bingos, and occasionally an eager beaver will even attempt a blackout. The bingos are intended to encompass a four- to six-week period to give all the children who wish to participate time to read the five books required.

The essential components of the bingos are a large-size bulletin board with the student bingo sheet reproduced in large size, student bingo sheets, bookmarks to be given for the first book read by each child, notes for the parents to sign, and a certificate for those who bingo. Many people who use the bingos also award a prize for each child who bingos—usually a small toy or paperback book. Children seem to enjoy participating with or without the prize, but recognizing those that bingo by presenting them a certificate in an assembly or posting the bingo winners on a large bulletin board is gratifying to the students and also helps promote participation in a future bingo. Sometimes showing the bingo winners a movie related to the bingo they have just participated in makes an award that is enjoyed by the students.

GENERAL DIRECTIONS: First make the bulletin board. You may cut out pictures to fit each category or enlarge the bulletin board squares which are included in this book. Enlarge them to a size appropriate for your bulletin board and then mount them on squares of construction paper and place them on the bulletin board in the exact format as the student bingo sheet. Above the bulletin board, using cut-out or plastic pin-back letters, spell out the name of the reading bingo which you are using. Then announce to the class or classes the rules for the bingo, making sure that they understand that all can win and that in order to win a student must read five books in a straight line on the bingo sheet, either horizontally, vertically, or diagonally. Tell them that after reading a book they are to take home a note for their parents to sign stating the name of the book and the student's name. (Note forms are provided in this book.) After the student returns the first note, give him/her their bingo sheet. To mark the square for the book which the child has read, use either a sticker or stamp with a rubber stamp. (A great variety of both stickers and rubber stamps are available and one can usually be found which will be appropriate to the bingo.) It is best to either post the bingo sheets or, if you do not have room to do this, keep the bingo sheets in a folder. If the bingo is being played in the library or media center, have a folder for each grade reading in the bingo. After the child has read his second book in the bingo, give him/her a bookmark appropriate to the bingo. (These bookmarks are in the book for you to duplicate, or provide one of your own if you prefer.)

When the first student completes a bingo, post that student's name somewhere on the bulletin board. Each subsequent student who bingos should also have his or her name posted on the bulletin board, or if there is not room post the names somewhere else in the room so that other students may see it.

At the end of the allotted time for the bingo, award the prizes in a school assembly, the media center, or the classroom. It is fun to take pictures of all the bingo winners and post them where other students may see them. This recognition will not only be gratifying to the winners, but also it will encourage others to participate in later bingos.

DIRECTIONS FOR AUTUMN READING BINGOS

Choose the bingo which you want to use for Autumn. If you choose SHARE A SCARE READING BINGO, you may wish to have your bingo run from the end of September until just before or just after Halloween. If you choose OUR AMERICAN HERITAGE READING BINGO, you may wish to have it run during November to capitalize on the history emphasis usually placed on the Thanksgiving holiday. OUR CANADIAN HERITAGE would be appropriate if used in Canada during October since their Thanksgiving holiday falls at that time. If it is used in the United States, it could be used during a time when a class might be studying Canada in their Social Studies classes.

See the general directions at the beginning of this unit for specific directions on how to run the bingos.

For the SHARE A SCARE READING BINGO, the student's bingo cards could be marked with a rubber stamp of a spider, ghost, bat, black cat, footprints, etc. OUR AMERICAN HERITAGE bingo sheets could be marked with the rubber stamp of an American flag, the liberty bell, or another patriotic symbol. OUR CANADIAN HERITAGE bingo sheets could be marked with a rubber stamp of the Canadian flag, the national animal (a beaver), or another patriotic symbol.

Stickers can also be used instead of rubber stamps. The stickers are colorful and attractive but they are more expensive, so in the case of a media center or library where many children might participate, the rubber stamp is probably more practical.

Enlarge each square for the bingo you have chosen using the designs included in this book, or you can, of course, create your own squares using cut-out colored pictures for each square. After enlarging the squares, mount them on an appropriately colored, slightly larger square of construction paper and then staple each square to the bulletin board in the exact pattern of the student bingo sheet. Ten

A. Autumn Reading Bingos

different types of books are included for each bingo and they will appear a different number of times in the bingo. You will therefore have to enlarge some of the pictures more than once so that you will have 25 squares for the bingo.

NUMBER OF SQUARES NEEDED FOR EACH AUTUMN BINGO:

SHARE A SCARE READING BINGO:

> 1 each of: "A Fiction Book About a Fire, Flood, or Storm" and "Snakes, Alligators, or Sharks"—Nonfiction. 2 each of: "A Disaster," "A Dangerous Animal," "A Maybe Monster," and "A Frightening Adventure"—Fiction. 3 each of: "A Halloween Book" and " A Ghost Story." 4 of: "A Fiction Mystery." 5 each of: "Your Choice of a Scary Book."

OUR AMERICAN HERITAGE READING BINGO:

> 2 each of: "Western Pioneers," "An American President," "American Explorers," "An Early American"—Nonfiction, "An American Artist or Author"—Nonfiction, and "An American Entertainer"—Nonfiction. 3 each of: "American Minorities," "An American Inventor," and "Early America." 4 each of: "American Historical Fiction."

OUR CANADIAN HERITAGE READING BINGO:

> 2 each of: "Western Pioneers," "A Canadian Prime Minister," "Our Heritage from France," "An Early Canadian," "A Canadian Artist or Author," and "A Canadian Entertainer or Sports Figure." 3 each of: "Our Heritage from England," "A Canadian Inventor*," and "Early Canada." 4 of: "Canadian Historical Fiction."

*A telephone is used because although Alexander Graham Bell's first working telephone was in the United States, he was born in Canada and experimented there.

SHARE A SCARE BINGO

WE LOVE TO BE SCARED!
READ ABOUT SOMETHING THAT FRIGHTENS YOU

A GHOST STORY	A BOOK ABOUT A DANGEROUS ANIMAL	FIRE, FLOOD OR STORM (FICTION)	YOUR CHOICE OF A "SCARY" BOOK	HALLOWEEN
HALLOWEEN	FICTION MYSTERY	SNAKES, SHARKS, OR ALLIGATORS	A GHOST STORY	YOUR CHOICE OF A "SCARY" BOOK
A "MAYBE" MONSTER (LOCH NESS, BIGFOOT, ETC.)	A DISASTER	YOUR CHOICE OF A "SCARY" BOOK	FICTION MYSTERY	FRIGHTENING ADVENTURE
YOUR CHOICE OF A "SCARY" BOOK	FRIGHTENING ADVENTURE	A "MAYBE" MONSTER (LOCH NESS, BIGFOOT, ETC.)	A DANGEROUS ANIMAL	A FICTION MYSTERY
A FICTION MYSTERY	YOUR CHOICE OF A "SCARY" BOOK	A GHOST STORY	HALLOWEEN	A DISASTER

© 1989 by The Center for Applied Research in Education

Record the titles of the books you have read in the appropriate square or on the back of this page.

Name _____ **Grade** _____

A GHOST STORY

HALLOWEEN

A FICTION MYSTERY

A "MAYBE" MONSTER

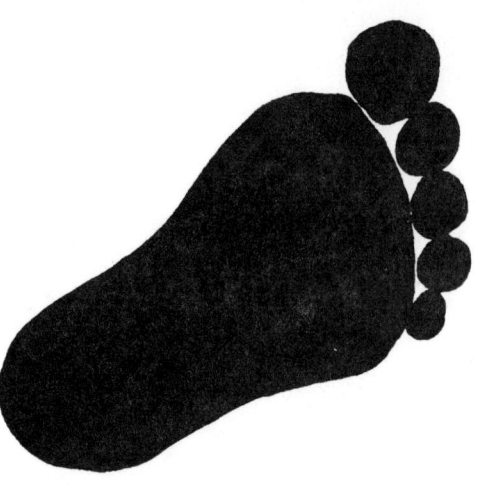

© 1989 by The Center for Applied Research in Education

YOUR CHOICE!

MYSTERIES, GHOST TALES, ADVENTURES, DISASTERS, WILD ANIMALS,

BOO! TALES TO SCARE YOU by...

A DISASTER
NONFICTION

A FRIGHTENING ADVENTURE

A FIRE, FLOOD, OR STORM

SNAKES, SHARKS, OR ALLIGATORS

A DANGEROUS ANIMAL

I LOVE A MYSTERY BOOK!

I LOVE A BOOK THAT SCARES ME!

WHOOO LIKES A BOOK THAT SCARES YOU?

I LIKE TO READ A GHOST STORY BOO!

© 1989 by The Center for Applied Research in Education

NOTE FROM HOME
_____
has read the book:
_____
for the SHARE A SCARE READING BINGO.
....
(Signature of parent or another responsible adult)

NOTE FROM HOME
_____
has read the book:
_____
for the SHARE A SCARE READING BINGO.
....
(Signature of parent or another responsible adult)

THIS CERTIFIES THAT

_____

HAS COMPLETED A BINGO IN THE

SHARE A SCARE READING BINGO

_____
SIGNATURE OF LIBRARIAN OR TEACHER

THIS CERTIFIES THAT

_____

HAS COMPLETED A BINGO IN THE

SHARE A SCARE READING BINGO

_____
SIGNATURE OF LIBRARIAN OR TEACHER

OUR AMERICAN HERITAGE
READING BINGO

AMERICAN MINORITIES (NONFICTION)	WESTERN PIONEERS (FICTION)	AMERICAN INVENTOR (NONFICTION)	AMERICAN HISTORICAL (FICTION)	AN AMERICAN PRESIDENT (NONFICTION)
AMERICAN EXPLORERS (NONFICTION)	EARLY AMERICA (FICTION)	AN EARLY AMERICAN (NONFICTION)	AN AMERICAN ARTIST OR WRITER (NONFICTION)	AN AMERICAN ENTERTAINER OR SPORTS FIGURE (NONFICTION)
AN AMERICAN INVENTOR (NONFICTION)	AMERICAN HISTORICAL (FICTION)	AMERICAN MINORITIES (NONFICTION)	EARLY AMERICA (FICTION)	WESTERN PIONEERS (FICTION)
EARLY AMERICA (FICTION)	AN AMERICAN PRESIDENT (NONFICTION)	AMERICAN HISTORICAL (FICTION)	AMERICAN EXPLORERS (NONFICTION)	AN EARLY AMERICAN (NONFICTION)
AMERICAN HISTORICAL (FICTION)	AMERICAN MINORITIES (NONFICTION)	AN AMERICAN ENTERTAINER OR SPORTS FIGURE (NONFICTION)	AN AMERICAN INVENTOR (NONFICTION)	AN AMERICAN ARTIST OR WRITER (NONFICTION)

Record the titles of the books you have read in the appropriate square or on the back of this page.

Name _____ **Grade** _____

© 1989 by The Center for Applied Research in Education

AMERICAN MINORITIES

CONTRIBUTIONS OF:
HISPANIC,
INDIAN
BLACK, AND
ORIENTAL
AMERICANS

HISTORICAL FICTION

MY BROTHER SAM IS DEAD,
WITCH OF BLACKBIRD POND,
LITTLE HOUSE ON THE PRAIRIE,
ON TO OREGON,
ETC.

EARLY AMERICA

FICTION

AN EARLY AMERICAN

READ ABOUT
DOLLY MADISON
NATHAN HALE
SAM ADAMS
JOHN ADAMS
PAUL REVERE
DEBORAH SAMPSON
ETC.

NONFICTION

© 1989 by The Center for Applied Research in Education

WESTERN PIONEERS

FICTION

American Inventor

AN AMERICAN PRESIDENT

AMERICAN EXPLORERS

NONFICTION

© 1989 by The Center for Applied Research in Education

AMERICAN ARTIST OR WRITER

AMERICAN ENTERTAINER OR SPORTS FIGURE

AMERICAN HERITAGE READING BINGO

OUR AMERICAN HERITAGE IN THE ARTS
READ!

READ ABOUT EARLY AMERICANS
AMERICAN HERITAGE BINGO

READ ABOUT AMERICAN INVENTORS AND INVENTIONS

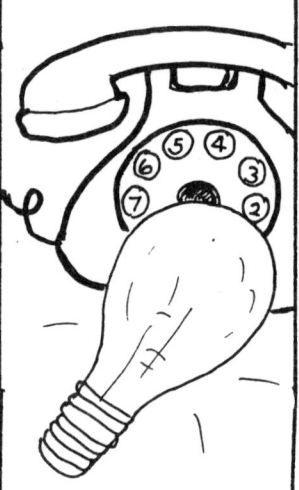

© 1989 by The Center for Applied Research in Education

NOTE FROM HOME

_____
(Child's Name)

HAS READ THE BOOK:

_____

FOR THE AMERICAN HERITAGE READING BINGO

....
(Signature of parent or another responsible adult)

NOTE FROM HOME

_____
(Child's Name)

HAS READ THE BOOK:

_____

FOR THE AMERICAN HERITAGE READING BINGO

....
(Signature of parent or another responsible adult)

THIS CERTIFIES THAT

_____

HAS COMPLETED A BINGO IN THE

AMERICAN HERITAGE READING BINGO

_____
Signature of teacher or librarian

© 1989 by The Center for Applied Research in Education

THIS CERTIFIES THAT

_____

HAS COMPLETED A BINGO IN THE

AMERICAN HERITAGE READING BINGO

_____
Signature of teacher or librarian

OUR CANADIAN HERITAGE
READING BINGO

OUR HERITAGE FROM ENGLAND (NONFICTION)	WESTERN PIONEERS (FICTION)	CANADIAN INVENTOR (NONFICTION)	CANADIAN HISTORICAL (FICTION)	A CANADIAN PRIME MINISTER (NONFICTION)
OUR HERITAGE FROM FRANCE (FICTION)	EARLY CANADA (FICTION)	AN EARLY CANADIAN (NONFICTION)	A CANADIAN ARTIST OR AUTHOR (NONFICTION)	A CANADIAN ENTERTAINER OR SPORTS FIGURE (NONFICTION)
CANADIAN INVENTOR (NONFICTION)	CANADIAN HISTORICAL (FICTION)	OUR HERITAGE FROM FRANCE (NONFICTION)	EARLY CANADA (FICTION)	WESTERN PIONEERS (FICTION)
EARLY CANADA (FICTION	A CANADIAN PRIME MINISTER (NONFICTION)	CANADIAN HISTORICAL (FICTION)	OUR HERITAGE FROM ENGLAND (NONFICTION)	AN EARLY CANADIAN (NONFICTION)
CANADIAN HISTORICAL (FICTION)	OUR HERITAGE FROM ENGLAND (NONFICTION)	A CANADIAN ENTERTAINER OR SPORTS FIGURE (NONFICTION)	A CANADIAN INVENTOR (NONFICTION)	A CANADIAN ARTIST OR WRITER (NONFICTION)

Name_____ Grade_____

© 1989 by The Center for Applied Research in Education

OUR HERITAGE FROM ENGLAND

OUR HERITAGE FROM FRANCE

WESTERN PIONEERS

EARLY CANADA

A CANADIAN PRIME MINISTER

Canadian Inventor or Scientist

AN EARLY CANADIAN

READ ABOUT:
John Cabot
Jacques Cartier
George Cartier
John MacDonald

HISTORICAL FICTION

I LIKE HISTORICAL FICTION!

CANADIAN ARTIST OR AUTHOR

CANADIAN ENTERTAINER OR SPORTS FIGURE

CANADIAN HERITAGE

READING BINGO

OUR CANADIAN HERITAGE IN THE ARTS

READ!

READ ABOUT EARLY CANADIANS

CANADIAN HERITAGE BINGO

READ ABOUT A CANADIAN ARTIST OR WRITER

© 1989 by The Center for Applied Research in Education

NOTE FROM HOME

_____
(Child's Name)

HAS READ THE BOOK:

_____

FOR THE CANADIAN
HERITAGE READING BINGO

....
(Signature of parent or another
 responsible adult)

NOTE FROM HOME

_____
(Child's Name)

HAS READ THE BOOK:

_____

FOR THE CANADIAN
HERITAGE READING BINGO

....
(Signature of parent or another
 responsible adult)

THIS CERTIFIES THAT

_____

**HAS COMPLETED A BINGO IN THE
CANADIAN HERITAGE**

READING BINGO

_____

SIGNATURE OF TEACHER OR LIBRARIAN

THIS CERTIFIES THAT

_____

**HAS COMPLETED A BINGO IN THE
CANADIAN HERITAGE**

READING BINGO

_____

SIGNATURE OF TEACHER OR LIBRARIAN

B. Autumn Student Detective Activities

DIRECTIONS FOR USE OF STUDENT DETECTIVE ACTIVITIES

Student Detective* activities are suitable for children who need more difficult library skills activities since they involve decision making as to which reference book to use. Often the activity involves the use of several different types of reference sources. They are suitable for advanced or gifted groups of children. Children who like a challenge will enjoy them, and these children can usually do the activities independently. The activities can be used in a classroom situation also, by going through the directions with the entire class and then deciding together which reference should be used for each clue.

The activities also make good media center or library contests. The librarian can introduce the student detective activities at the beginning of the year and explain to the children that they represent a contest, but that all may win by doing the activity in their free time. All who complete the activity are winners. Winners can be given certificates (provided in this book) or a small prize such as a pencil, bookmark, sticker, etc. It makes others want to do the activities if the first winners are honored by having their names posted on a bulletin board or by recognizing them in an assembly.

The student detective activities in this book are for the different seasons so that you may use them several times during the year.

---

*Other Student Detective activities are available from QUAILRIDGE MEDIA, Selma, Oregon

TEACHER'S PAGE FOR
"THE STUDENT DETECTIVE AND THE CASE OF THE MISSING FOOTBALL"

THE STUDENT DETECTIVE AND THE CASE OF THE MISSING FOOTBALL is a good activity to use in September, October, or November. It is one of the easier Student Detective activities since all the clues can be answered by using either the encyclopedia or the almanac.

REFERENCES USED IN SOLVING THIS ACTIVITY:

1. Almanac
2. Encyclopedia (or Almanac)
3. Almanac
4. Encyclopedia
5. Almanac
6. Almanac
7. Encyclopedia
8. Almanac
9. Encyclopedia
10. Encyclopedia

KEY: The football was taken by *Paul Jackson*. His address was *159 O'Connor* Street. He took it to his grandma's house in *Portland*. Her address was *907 Calhoun* Street. The boy said he'd bring the football back to them on *Saturday, June 10th*.

THIS ACTIVITY WAS USED WITH:

_____ CLASS on _____ (date)

NOTES:_____

STUDENT DETECTIVE AND THE CASE OF THE MISSING FOOTBALL

The kids on Anne Street were all set for a game of touch football, but no one could find the ball!

Dan said that he had had it yesterday but he had given it to Bob. Bob said that he gave it to Eden, and Eden insisted that she'd seen Lori with it last.

It was a beautiful day and all the kids wanted to play, so they called the Student Detective to help them find the ball. The Student Detective solved the case and found the football. Can you solve this case too? Follow the clues and put your answer in the blanks below the clues.

THE CLUES:

1. The football was taken by a boy whose first name is the same as the Nobel Prize winner for Chemistry in 1974.
2. The boy's last name is the same as that of the seventh President of the United States.
3. The boy lives at a house whose house number is the same as the number of counties in the state of Georgia.
4. The house is on a street with the same name as the last name of the first woman to ever be appointed to the Supreme Court of the United States.
5. The boy didn't see a name on the football so he took it with him to his Grandma's house. She lived in a city where the NBA basketball team, the TRAILBLAZERS play.
6. Grandma's house number is the same as the area code number for Alaska.
7. Her street has the same name as the last name of the Vice-President under President John Quincy Adams.
8. The Student Detective called the boy at his grandmother's house. The boy said he would bring the football back on the same day of the week that Christmas will fall on in 1999.
9. The date will be in the same month as the month when Flag Day is celebrated.
10. The day of the month will be the same as the number of provinces in Canada.

YOUR ANSWERS TO THE CASE OF THE MISSING FOOTBALL:

The football was taken by _____ _____. His address was
                              1.   2.
a _____ _____ Street. He took the football to his grandma's
      3.   4.
house in _____. Her address was _____ _____.
              5.   6.   7.
The boy said he'd bring the football back on _____, _____ _____. The
                                                  8.   9.   10.
kids played soccer until the football was brought back!

Name_____   Grade_____

© 1989 by The Center for Applied Research in Education

_____

is awarded the title of:

Super Student Detective

for solving the case of

THE CASE OF THE MISSING FOOTBALL

_____
Signature of teacher or librarian

_____ (date)

_____

is awarded the title of:

Super Student Detective

for solving the case of

THE CASE OF THE MISSING FOOTBALL

_____
Signature of teacher or librarian

_____ (date)

TEACHER'S PAGE FOR "THE STUDENT DETECTIVE AND THE CASE OF THE MISSING MARCHING BAND"

THE STUDENT DETECTIVE AND THE CASE OF THE MISSING MARCHING BAND is about a band which is missing in a Veteran's Day parade so it would be especially appropriate in either late October or early November. This activity is a little more difficult than the first one since it uses several more reference sources. The almanac, dictionary, encyclopedia, and *The Guinness Book of Records* are all used in solving this activity.

REFERENCES USED IN SOLVING THIS ACTIVITY:

1. Almanac
2. Encyclopedia
3. Almanac
4. Almanac
5. Dictionary
6. *Guinness Book of World Records* (1985 edition—answer could be different in later editions.)
7. Almanac
8. Dictionary
9. Almanac

KEY: The band was to meet at *Fleming* Park. The Student Detective figured the band might be at another park, so he looked in *Borglum* Park and then on *Bancroft* Street in *Waterman* Park. The band was found in this last park. They were all standing next to the park's *collection of wild animals (or zoo)*. The Student Detective directed the band to the right park which was between *Pollock* (Mrs. Alice Pollock, age 102 years 8 months 1987 *Guinness Book of World Records*) Street and *Huey P. Long* Street. When the band arrived everything was in an *uproar*, but everyone was happy when the band arrived and the parade finally began at *10* a.m.

ACTIVITY USED by _____ class on _____ (Date)

NOTES: _____

THE STUDENT DETECTIVE AND THE CASE OF THE MISSING MARCHING BAND

The school marching band at Riverview Middle School was excited. They had been asked to march and play in the big Veteran's Day Parade. They were so excited that they forgot to listen carefully to the directions and on the day of the parade they were not where they were supposed to be. Everyone was ready for the parade to begin but the Riverview Marching Band was not there.

"We'll have to start without them," said the mayor. "Wait!" said the Student Detective who was standing nearby. Give me 20 minutes. CAN YOU SOLVE THE CLUES BELOW TO FIND THE BAND IN LESS THAN THE 20 MINUTES IT TOOK THE STUDENT DETECTIVE? TRY IT AND SEE!

CLUE #1: The Student Detective knew the band was to meet at the park whose name was the same as the last name of the winner of the women's figure skating in the 1968 Winter Olympics.

CLUE #2: The Student Detective figured the band had gone to another park so he looked in a park whose name was the same as the last name of the artist who designed the heads carved in Mt. Rushmore.

CLUE #3: The band was not in that park so the Student Detective went down a street whose name was the same as the last name of the Academy Award winner for best actress in 1962.

CLUE #4: At the end of this street was a park whose name was the same as the last name of the inventor of the fountain pen.

CLUE #5: The band was located in the park next to the *menagerie*.

CLUES #6 & 7: The Student Detective directed the band to the right park which was between the street whose name was the same as the last name of the person who was the world's oldest authoress and the street with the same name as the name of the world's longest railroad bridge.

CLUE #8: When the band arrived everything was in a *brouhaha*.

CLUE #9: The parade finally began at the same time in the morning as the number of counties in the state of New Hampshire.

PUT YOUR ANSWERS TO THE CLUES ABOVE IN THE SPACES BELOW:

The band was to meet at _____ Park. The Student Detective
                              (1)

figured the band might be at another park so he looked in _____ Park
                                                                (2)

and then on _____ Street in _____ Park. The band was found
              (3)   (4)

in this last park. They were all standing next to the park's _____.
                                                                    (5)

The Student Detective directed the band to the right park which was between

_____ Street and _____ Street. When the band arrived everything
    (6)   (7)

was in an _____, but everyone was happy when they saw the band
              (8)

and the parade finally begin at _____ a.m.
                                     (9)

Name _____   Grade _____

_____

is awarded the title of:

Super Student Detective

for solving

THE CASE OF THE MISSING
MARCHING BAND

_____
Signature of teacher or librarian

_____
(Date)

_____

is awarded the title of:

Super Student Detective

for solving

THE CASE OF THE MISSING
MARCHING BAND

_____
Signature of teacher or librarian

_____
(Date)

© 1989 by The Center for Applied Research in Education

C. Autumn Crossword Count Puzzles

DIRECTIONS FOR USING CROSSWORD COUNT PUZZLES

CROSSWORD COUNT PUZZLES* are fun to use in either a classroom or a library/media center situation.

In the classroom use them as a challenge to see if the students can beat the previous high count record for that crossword count puzzle. (A chart to keep the record scores from year to year is provided with the crossword count puzzles.)

DIRECTIONS:

In each puzzle the students are to enter words in the spaces provided. Sometimes the words will go horizontally, such as in BACK TO SCHOOL CROSSWORD COUNT, A PILGRIM THANKSGIVING CROSSWORD COUNT, FUN IN THE SNOW CROSSWORD COUNT, and THE LUCK OF THE IRISH CROSSWORD COUNT. At other times the words are to go around the square, both horizontally and vertically, such as in CUPID—A VALENTINE CROSSWORD COUNT, WELCOME SPRING CROSSWORD COUNT, and A BUSY TIME FOR BEES CROSSWORD COUNT.

The students try to achieve high scores by using the dictionary to find words containing high point letters. The letter count for each puzzle is listed beside the puzzle. Each puzzle contains different point counts for each letter with the letters in the featured word having the highest count. After the students are satisfied with the words they have chosen (any word is acceptable if it is in the dictionary except proper nouns and abbreviations), they enter the point count of each letter in the spaces at the bottom of the page. They then total their scores up to see who has the highest count.

In a classroom situation you might let two students work together with the dictionary for an assigned time, such as 20 minutes. At the end of the time, the pair of students or the individual student with the highest score is the winner. You may wish to challenge them to beat the highest score of the previous year.

In a media center or library the puzzle can be run as a month-long contest with the two highest scores in each grade awarded a certificate (provided in this book) or a small prize such as a bookmark, special eraser, or pencil.

NOTES:_____

_____

_____

*Other Crossword Count Puzzles are available from QUAILRIDGE MEDIA, Selma, Oregon.

RECORD OF SCORES FOR AUTUMN CROSSWORD COUNT PUZZLES

BACK-TO-SCHOOL CROSSWORD COUNT

YEAR	GRADE IN SCHOOL	SCORE	PERSON ACHIEVING THE SCORE

A PILGRIM THANKSGIVING CROSSWORD COUNT

YEAR	GRADE IN SCHOOL	SCORE	PERSON ACHIEVING THE SCORE

© 1989 by The Center for Applied Research in Education

BACK-TO-SCHOOL CROSSWORD COUNT

See how many points you can get in this back-to-school crossword count. The words you use should go from left to right as the word "school" does. Use the dictionary and try to use words which have letters with a high point count. You do not need to make words going up and down. Do not use proper nouns in your puzzle. GOOD LUCK!

POINT COUNT FOR LETTERS

A = 6
B = 5
C = 25
D = 22
E = 17
F = 19
G = 2
H = 24
I = 12
J = 4
K = 10
L = 21
M = 11
N = 13
O = 23
P = 14
Q = 7
R = 15
S = 26
T = 20
U = 9
V = 8
W = 16
X = 1
Y = 18
Z = 3

Put your point count for each letter in the space below. Then add up your total.

Box 1:____ Box 2:____ Box 3:____ Box 4:____ Box 5:____ Box 6:____

Box 7:____ Box 8:____ Box 9:____ Box 10:____ Box 11:____ Box 12:____

Box 13:____ Box 14:____ Box 15:____ Box 16:____ Box 17:____ Box 18:____

Box 19:____ Box 20:____ Box 21:____ Box 22:____ Box 23:____ Box 24:____

Name_____ Grade_____

_____

HAS WON FIRST PLACE IN THE

Back to School

CROSSWORD COUNT CONTEST.

_____
TEACHER/LIBRARIAN

DATE: _____

_____

HAS WON SECOND PRIZE IN THE

Back to School

CROSSWORD COUNT CONTEST.

_____
TEACHER/LIBRARIAN

DATE: _____

© 1989 by The Center for Applied Research in Education

A PILGRIM THANKSGIVING
CROSSWORD COUNT

Use the dictionary to find words which contain high point letters. Put the words in the puzzle below. See if you can score the highest point count.

REMEMBER: Words go across (horizontally) the puzzle. They cannot be proper nouns.

GOOD LUCK!

LETTER POINT COUNT
A = 20
B = 19
C = 18
D = 16
E = 17
F = 11
G = 23
H = 15
I = 25
J = 5
K = 10
L = 24
M = 21
N = 14
O = 4
P = 26
Q = 1
R = 22
S = 13
T = 12
U = 9
V = 8
W = 7
X = 2
Y = 6
Z = 3

YOUR POINT COUNT: Box 1:____ Box 2:____ Box 3:____ Box 4:____

Box 5:____ Box 6:____ Box 7:____ Box 8:____ Box 9:____ Box 10:____

Box 11:____ Box 12:____ Box 13:____ Box 14:____ Box 15:____ Box 16:____

Box 17:____ Box 18:____ TOTAL SCORE:____

MY TOTAL SCORE IS: _____

Name_____ Grade_____

1st

_____

HAS WON FIRST PLACE IN THE

A Pilgrim Thanksgiving

CROSSWORD COUNT CONTEST.

_____
TEACHER/LIBRARIAN

DATE: _____

2nd

_____

HAS WON SECOND PRIZE IN THE

A Pilgrim Thanksgiving

CROSSWORD COUNT CONTEST.

_____
TEACHER/LIBRARIAN

DATE: _____

© 1989 by The Center for Applied Research in Education

D. Research Activities for Autumn

TEACHER'S PAGE AND KEY FOR "RESEARCH BINGO FOR AUTUMN"

In this activity children may bingo by answering five questions in any straight row, vertically, horizontally, or diagonally. In a classroom situation students may be assigned the direction they are to go for their bingo. In this way there will not be overcrowding in any section of the reference section. Students enjoy being timed and you could put the time of each student on their paper as they bingo.

In the media center or library, the activity could also be used as a voluntary activity, again letting students bingo by answering any five questions in a straight line. Names of students who bingo could be posted and pictures taken of all the winners. All students should be allowed to bingo, not just the first ones in any direction.

Another interest-grabbing way to use the activity is to enlarge each square and mount it on the bulletin board in an exact replica of the bingo card. Then, as students bingo, their names could be put beside the bingo card on the bulletin board, and a colored yarn or string could be pinned from the student's name across the bingo board in the direction that student scored his/her bingo.

KEY:
1. Varies according to collection but should be a book about football   2. 44070   3. Joan Blos   4. Varies depending on the dictionary used   5. Marc Brown   6. Lake Placid, New York   7. o tum n 1   8. 97132   9. Zilpha Snyder   10. Richard Nixon   11. Rene Cassin   12. Varies according to your collection but should be a book containing plays and scripts   13. Varies according to dictionary used   14. Thomas R. Marshall   15. Theodore Taylor   16. Lynn Reid Banks   17. Susan Cooper   18. Morrow Company   19. 68801   20. Varies according to your collection but should be a book about cats or kittens   21. ouphe, barghest, bogle   22. 1974   23. 68310   24. Varies according to collection, but should be any book title about a fairytale or folktale   25. Meryl Streep

RESEARCH BINGO

FOR AUTUMN

Fill in the answers in five squares in a straight line. Your squares may be vertical, horizontal, or diagonal.

1. Write the title of a book which has a number of 796.33. _____ _____	2. What is the zip code for North Olmsted, Ohio? _____	3. Who won the Newbery medal in 1980? _____	4. What are the guide words on the dictionary page with the word "Autumn"? _____ and _____	5. Who is the author of *Arthur's Halloween*? _____
6. Where the 1980 Winter Olympics were held? _____	7. How do you pronounce the word "Autumnal"? _____	8. What is the zip code of Newberg, Oregon? _____	9. Who wrote *The Egypt Game*? _____	10. Who was the Vice-President during President Eisenhower's first term? _____
11. Who won the 1968 Nobel Prize for Peace? _____	12. What is the title of any book with the call number 808.2? _____	13. What are the guide words on the dictionary page where the word "fall" is found? _____ and _____	14. Who was the Vice-President for President Woodrow Wilson? _____	15. Who wrote *The Cay*? _____
16. Who wrote *The Indian in the Cupboard*? _____	17. Who won the Newbery Medal in 1976? _____	18. Who is the publisher of *Ramona, the Pest*? _____	19. What is the zip code of Grand Island, Nebraska? _____	20. What is the title of any book with a call number of 636.8? _____
21. What is a synonym for the word goblin? _____	22. What is the copyright date for *Where the Sidewalk Ends*? _____	23. What is the zip code for Beatrice, Nebraska? _____	24. What is the title for any book with a call number of 398.2? _____	25. Who won the Academy Award for best actress in 1982? _____

Name_____ Date_____

© 1989 by The Center for Applied Research in Education

D. Research Activities for Autumn

TEACHER'S PAGE FOR "THE COLORS OF AUTUMN"

The activities for "The Colors of Autumn" page are card catalog activities. The sheet could be used in different ways. One way would be to copy the page so that each student had a copy. Then all the students would use the card catalog to locate the authors and all numbers for each title. Students who complete the page could look on the shelves to try to find other books which have a title containing the Autumn colors of gold, brown, red, orange, and yellow.

Another way to use the page is to copy it on orange paper. Mount the pumpkins on a 3" × 4" black cardboard and then laminate. Have a pumpkin card for each student who must then locate the title in the card catalog, write the author's name and call number (this could be on another sheet of paper, or give each student a marking pencil or pen and let him or her write on the laminated card), and then find the book.

A page of pumpkins with no titles on them is provided so that you make additional pumpkins with titles to match your collection.

Other titles which could be used are: *The Red Balloon* by Lamorisse, *Red Cloud* by Garst, *Red is Best* by Stinson, *The Red Room Riddle* by Scott Corbett, *Red Tag Comes Back* by Phleger, *The Yellow Brick Toad* by Mike Thaler, *The Golden Goblet* by Eloise McGraw, *Where the Red Fern Grows* by Rawls, *The Big Orange Drawing Book* by Ed Emberley, *Oh, the Red Rose Tree* by Patricia Beatty, *Golden Mare* by William Corbin, *The Red Badge of Courage* by Stephen Crane, *The Red Tape Gang* by Nixon, *Mystery at the Red House* by Meigs.

The above are but a few of the many titles with the Autumn colors in them.

The page with the blank pumpkins could also be used to write titles of Halloween books. The students could use the card catalog to write the call slips for the books and then find the books. This would be a good way to get the Halloween books pulled for display early in October.

THE KEY: *The City of Gold and Lead* by John Christopher, *The Mystery of the Flying Orange Pumpkin* by Stephen Kellogg, *Black Gold* by Marguerite Henry, *The Big Orange Splot* by Daniel Pinkwater, *Big Red* by Jim Kjelgaard, *Brown Bear, Brown Bear* by Bill Martin, *The Yellow House Mystery* by Gertrude Chandler Warner, *The Golden Egg Book* by Margaret Brown, *Little Red Riding Hood* by (Many authors have rewritten this story so the author will depend on your collection.)

All call numbers will depend on how your library collection is arranged.

THE COLORS OF AUTUMN

Use the card catalog to help you find these books whose titles contain one of the Autumn colors of orange, red, gold, brown, or yellow. If your card catalog does not contain these titles, perhaps your teacher has a copy of *Books in Print* or *Children's Books in Print* which you could use.

THE CITY OF GOLD AND LEAD
Author:
Call Number:

THE MYSTERY OF THE FLYING ORANGE PUMPKIN
Author:
Call Number:

BLACK GOLD
Author:
Call Number:

THE BIG ORANGE SPLOT
Author:
Call Number:

BIG RED
Author:
Call Number:

BROWN BEAR, BROWN BEAR
Author:
Call Number:

THE YELLOW HOUSE MYSTERY
Author:
Call Number:

THE GOLDEN EGG BOOK
Author:
Call Number:

LITTLE RED RIDING HOOD
Author:
Call Number:

Name _____ Date _____

D. Research Activities for Autumn

TEACHER'S PAGE FOR "IT HAPPENED IN THE AUTUMN"

GRADE LEVELS: 5–8

SKILLS: Following Directions, Research skills in card catalog, encyclopedia, and almanac

This activity is a good one to use early in Autumn. It could be used with gifted classes or with academically capable classes by giving no help in deciding which reference book to use for each question and letting them follow the directions unaided. In average classes you may wish to go through the questions together deciding which reference source to use. You may also wish to do one together. Number 14 would be a good one to do together since most schools have enough almanacs so that each student or at least each two students may have an almanac to use. It would also be a good one to do together if the students have not previously used a perpetual calendar.

Have the children locate the answer by using the perpetual calendar in the almanac and then show them where to put the called-for letters in the blank spaces of the message.

Assign each student to a question to begin on, since this will relieve overcrowding at the card catalog or reference section. Be sure the students understand that they are to complete all of the questions and not just the one assigned to them to begin on.

Other activities could be for each student to write one other research question for an event which occurred in Autumn.

Able students could be given time in another session or as homework to prepare their own mystery message for their classmates to solve.

The message is: enjoy school and sports in Autumn.

KEY: 1. Charles Schulz   2. Samuel Clemens
3. Louisa May Alcott   4. Mrs. O'Leary   5. Pacific
6. Jimmy Carter   7. Eleanor   8. Russia   9. James Naismith
10. Robert Louis Stevenson   11. Pablo   12. Carlo Collodi
13. William Steig   14. Thursday   15. radium

NOTES: _____

IT HAPPENED IN THE AUTUMN

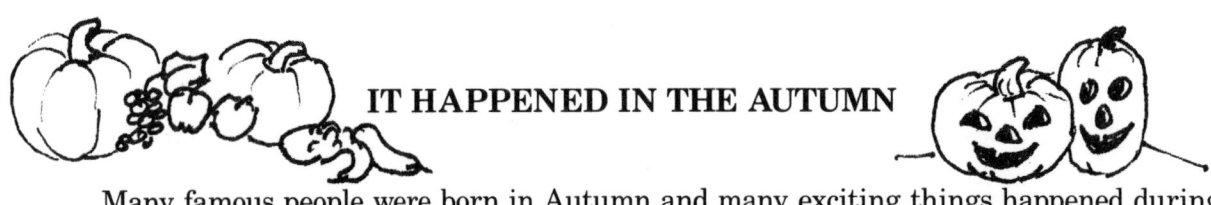

Many famous people were born in Autumn and many exciting things happened during this time of year. Answer these questions about things that happened in Autumn and then do what the directions say. If you read carefully, do your research well, and follow directions exactly, you will be able to figure out the secret message.

1. The famous creator of Charlie Brown and Snoopy was born on November 25th. His name is _____. Put the first letter of his first name on space 7.
2. Mark Twain, author of *The Adventures of Tom Sawyer* was born on November 30, 1835. Mark Twain is not his real name. What is it? _____ Put the 2nd letter of his last name in space 11.
3. The author of *Little Women* was born on November 29, 1832. Her name is _____. Put the first letter of her last name in spaces 12 and 23.
4. The Great Chicago Fire was in October of 1871. According to legend it was started by a cow kicking over a lantern. Whose cow was it? _____. Put the first letter of her last name in spaces 4, 9, 10, and 17.
5. On September 25th in 1513 explorer Balboa discovered a famous ocean. Which ocean was it? _____. Put the 4th letter of the name of that ocean in space 21.
6. Our 39th President was born on October 1, 1924. His name is _____. Put the first letter of his first name in space 3.
7. On October 11, 1884, the wife of President Franklin Roosevelt was born. What is her first name? _____. Put the 1st letter of her 1st name in space 1.
8. Alaska Day is celebrated in October because it was in October that Alaska was purchased by the United States from another country. That country was _____. Put the 2nd letter of that country's name in spaces 24 and 26.
9. The inventor of the game of basketball was born on November 6, 1861. His name is _____. Put the 1st letter of his last name in spaces 2, 13, 22, and 28. Put the 3rd letter of his first name in space 27.
10. The author of *Treasure Island* was born on November 13, 1850. His name is _____. Put the 2nd letter of his last name in spaces 19 and 25.
11. On October 28, 1881, the famous painter, Picasso, was born. What is his first name? _____. Put the 1st letter of his first name in space 16.
12. The author of *Pinocchio* was born on Nov. 24, 1826. His pen name is _____. Put the 6th letter of his last name in space 14.
13. The author of *Sylvester & the Magic Pebble* was born on Nov. 14, 1907. His name is _____. Put the 1st letter of his last name in spaces 6, 15 and 20.
14. Halloween is October 31st every year. On what day of the week will it fall in the year 2002? _____. Put the 2nd letter of that day in space 8. Put the last letter of that day in space 5.
15. Marie Curie was born on Nov. 7, 1867. She was the co-winner of a Nobel Prize for the discovery of _____. Put the 1st letter of that discovery in space 18. Put the last letter of that discovery in space 27.

```
__ __ __ __ __ __ __ __ __ __ __ __ __ __ __ __ __ __ __ __ __ __ __ __ __ __ __ __
 1  2  3  4  5  6  7  8  9 10 11 12 13 14 15 16 17 18 19 20 21 22 23 24 25 26 27 28
```

THE MESSAGE IS: _____

Name _____   Grade _____

© 1989 by The Center for Applied Research in Education

D. Research Activities for Autumn

TEACHER'S PAGE FOR "IN AUTUMN IT'S APPLE TIME!"

The very popular fruit, apples, makes a good research topic for Autumn. Often it works in with units in classroom reading textbooks. This activity involves using the encyclopedia, *The Guinness Book of Records, Famous First Facts*, the dictionary, and a book of famous quotations. Because of using so many reference sources it is probably best suited to students in grades 5 - 8, but it could be adapted for students in lower grades by leaving out questions 1, 2, and 9.

To prevent overcrowding in the reference section assign different beginning questions to each student. Explain to students that even though they begin on different questions, they are to answer *all* questions. Questions 3, 4, 5, 6, and 7 can be answered by using the encyclopedia, so, depending upon the number of sets in your media center/library, more could be assigned to those questions. Question 1 can be found in a book of quotations, question 2 in *The Guinness Book of World Records*, question 8 in a dictionary (probably a college or unabridged edition), and question 9 in *Famous First Facts*. Assign students to each question depending upon how many of each reference source is available. Question 10 is one that will be fun for the children and will keep the fast finishers busy while the slower students complete the activity.

KEY: 1. Anonymous.   2. V. Loveridge of Rosson-Wye, England grew a 3 lb., 1 oz. apple in 1965 (record still intact as of *1986 Guinness Book of Records*).   3. Russia (*1986 World Book Encyclopedia*).   4. Washington and New York (*1986 World Book*).   5. At least 2½ million (*1986 World Book*). 6. John Chapman born in 1774 in Leominster, Mass.   7. Newton discovered the law of gravity because of watching an apple fall from a tree (*1986 World Book*).   8. A "pome" is a fruit with a fleshy outer layer, a paperlike core, and more than one seed.   9. The apple parer was invented by Moses Coats, a mechanic from Downington, PA.   10. Some of the words which could be formed using letters from the word "apples" are: sap, pal, lap, slap, pale, pap, pep, ape.

NOTES:

IN AUTUMN IT'S APPLE TIME!

Apples are among the world's favorite fruits. In North America most apples ripen in September and October. Use your research skills to find out some interesting facts about apples.

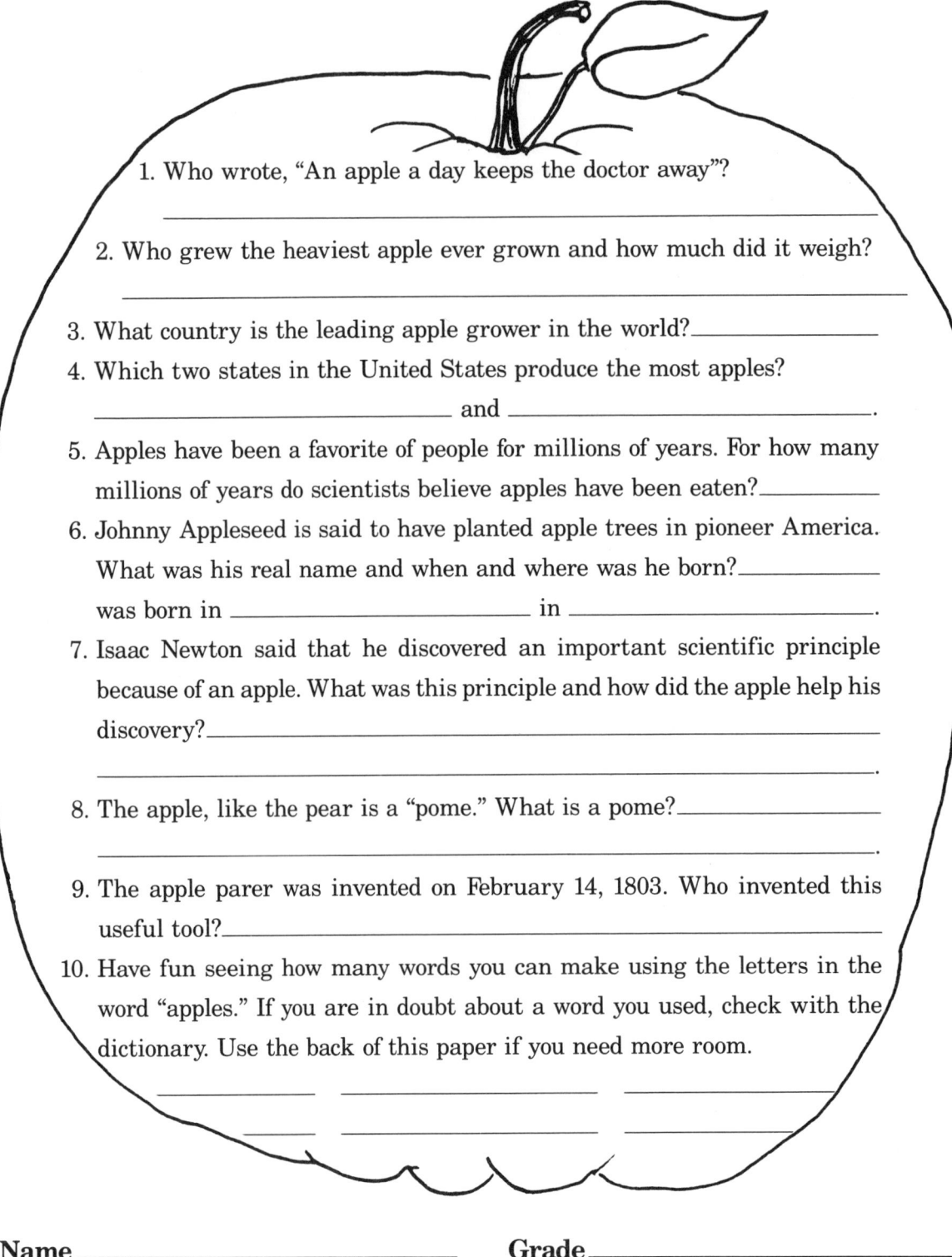

1. Who wrote, "An apple a day keeps the doctor away"? _____

2. Who grew the heaviest apple ever grown and how much did it weigh? _____

3. What country is the leading apple grower in the world?_____

4. Which two states in the United States produce the most apples? _____ and _____.

5. Apples have been a favorite of people for millions of years. For how many millions of years do scientists believe apples have been eaten?_____

6. Johnny Appleseed is said to have planted apple trees in pioneer America. What was his real name and when and where was he born?_____ was born in _____ in _____.

7. Isaac Newton said that he discovered an important scientific principle because of an apple. What was this principle and how did the apple help his discovery?_____
_____.

8. The apple, like the pear is a "pome." What is a pome?_____
_____.

9. The apple parer was invented on February 14, 1803. Who invented this useful tool?_____

10. Have fun seeing how many words you can make using the letters in the word "apples." If you are in doubt about a word you used, check with the dictionary. Use the back of this paper if you need more room.

_____ _____ _____
_____ _____ _____

Name_____ **Grade**_____

© 1989 by The Center for Applied Research in Education

D. Research Activities for Autumn

TEACHER'S PAGE FOR "ENCYCLOPEDIA RESEARCH ACTIVITIES FOR HALLOWEEN"

SUGGESTED GRADE LEVELS: 3 and 4

DIRECTIONS: The following six pages are for use as continuing work in the encyclopedia for third graders and any fourth graders who still need to become adept at using the encyclopedia. Some second graders could do this also. All six activities are meant to be used at the same time so that there will be enough encyclopedias for all. Assign each sheet to the number of children who can be accommodated by your number of encyclopedias. Most libraries have four to six or more sets, so if there were three to four children started on each activity there should be enough volumes for all. Volumes may be shared provided the students know that each student is to write his own sentences and fill in his own activity sheet. The activity could be used for several days with the students being given different activity sheets on subsequent days…example: the ghost on one day, the bat on another, etc. If you use the material in this way, able students could write a fiction story about their subject on the back of the activity sheet or illustrate their sentences on a piece of construction paper. They will need this extra activity since many will be finished before the class period is ended.

Another way to use the activity sheets is to let the students do several of the sheets in one day. This may make a little problem in having enough encyclopedia sets to accommodate the students. Save time at the end of each session to read the sentences each student wrote after reading their encyclopedia selection. If the students know that they are going to read their sentences to the class, most of them will take more care to write good sentences.

If there are students whose religion prevents them from doing Halloween activities, assign them the pumpkin or bat activities since these are not restricted to Halloween.

KEY: All answers will vary according to encyclopedia set used.

Did you dress up like a ghost on Halloween? Look up ghost in an encyclopedia. What is the name of the encyclopedia set you used? _____

In which volume did you find the entry for ghosts?_____

On which page did the article about ghosts begin?_____ What were the guide words on that page?_____ _____

Write one or two good sentences about ghosts. Use the information you found in the encyclopedia to write your sentences.

_____
_____
_____
_____
_____

© 1989 by The Center for Applied Research in Education

Name_____ **Grade**_____

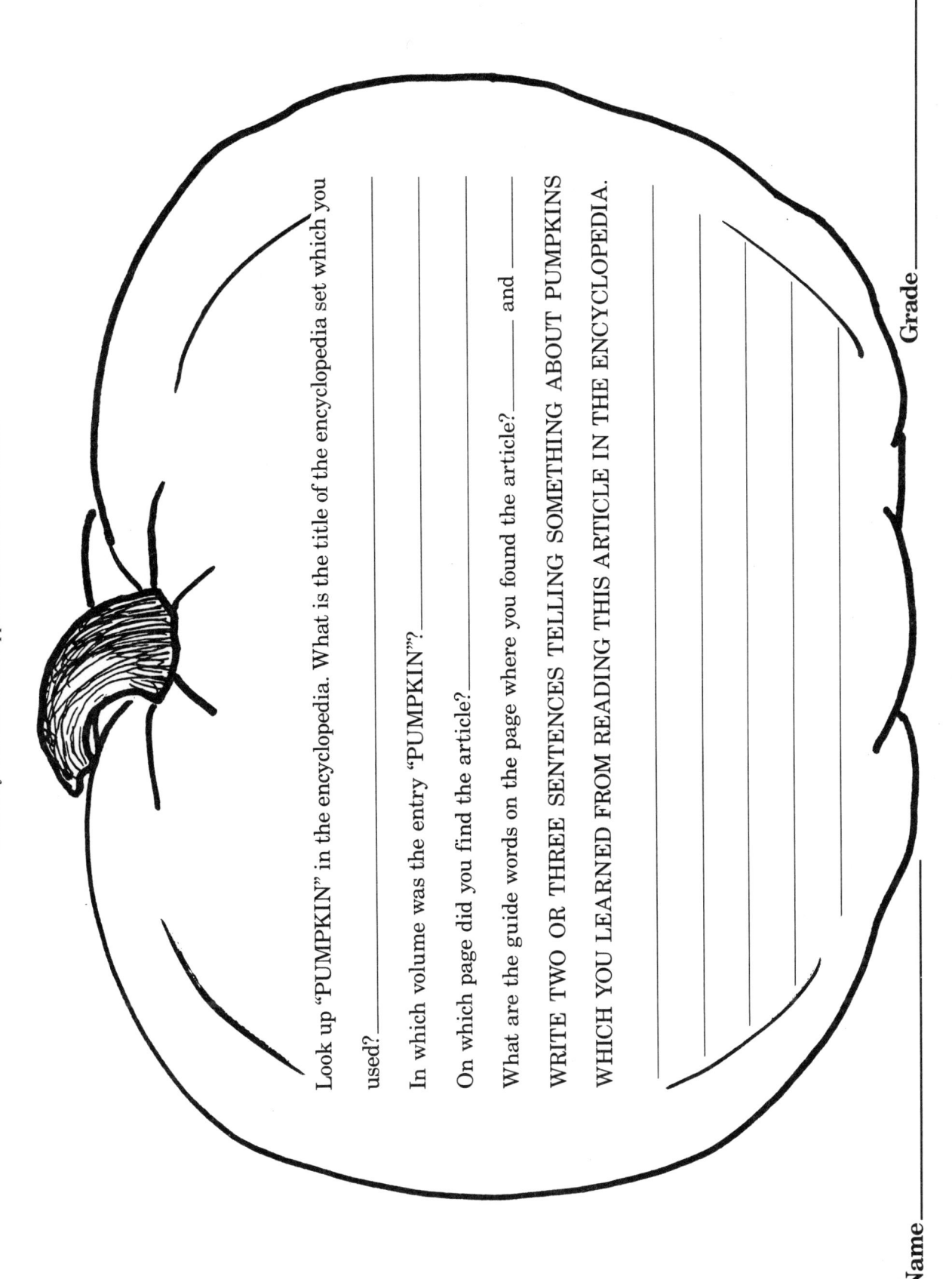

Look up "PUMPKIN" in the encyclopedia. What is the title of the encyclopedia set which you used? _____

In which volume was the entry "PUMPKIN"? _____

On which page did you find the article? _____

What are the guide words on the page where you found the article? _____ and _____

WRITE TWO OR THREE SENTENCES TELLING SOMETHING ABOUT PUMPKINS WHICH YOU LEARNED FROM READING THIS ARTICLE IN THE ENCYCLOPEDIA.

_____
_____
_____
_____
_____

Name _____   Grade _____

LOOK UP "BAT" IN THE ENCYCLOPEDIA.

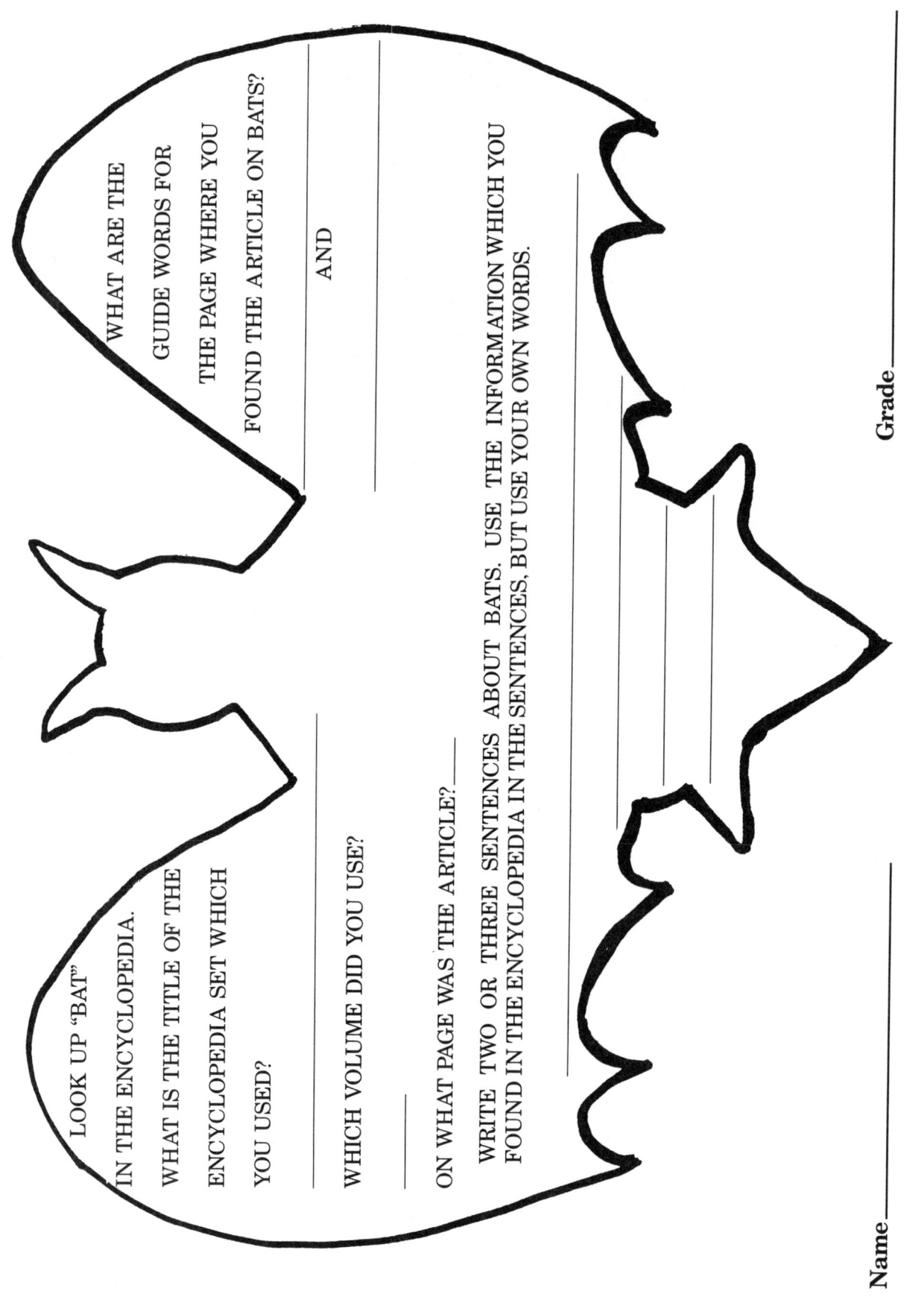

WHAT IS THE TITLE OF THE ENCYCLOPEDIA SET WHICH YOU USED? _____

WHICH VOLUME DID YOU USE? _____

ON WHAT PAGE WAS THE ARTICLE? _____

WRITE TWO OR THREE SENTENCES ABOUT BATS. USE THE INFORMATION WHICH YOU FOUND IN THE ENCYCLOPEDIA IN THE SENTENCES, BUT USE YOUR OWN WORDS.

_____
_____
_____

WHAT ARE THE GUIDE WORDS FOR THE PAGE WHERE YOU FOUND THE ARTICLE ON BATS?

_____ AND _____

Name _____ Grade _____

© 1989 by The Center for Applied Research in Education

Look up Halloween in an encyclopedia. Which set of encyclopedias did you use?_____ In which volume did you find "Halloween"?_____On which page was the entry for Halloween?_____What were the guide words on that page?_____Write a sentence or two telling something you learned from the article about Halloween.

_____
_____
_____
_____
_____

© 1989 by The Center for Applied Research in Education

Name_____ **Grade**_____

Black cats remind us of Halloween. Look up cats in an encyclopedia. Which encyclopedia set did you use? _____

In which volume did you find the entry for cats? ____ On which page did the article on cats begin?____ What are the guide words?____ and____ Write a sentence or two telling something you learned about cats by reading the encyclopedia._____
_____
_____
_____
_____
_____
_____

© 1989 by The Center for Applied Research in Education

Name_____ Grade_____

CAN YOU BEAT THE WITCH TO THE PUMPKIN PATCH? I

The old witch took 30 minutes to find all the answers to her Halloween questions. Can you beat her to the pumpkin patch by answering these questions in less than 30 minutes?

START HERE

1. What is an *obese* witch? _____ Make one by the pumpkin patch.

2. If a witch has long *tresses* what does she have? _____ Give the witch you made below long tresses.

3. Make one of the pumpkins below *crimson*.

4. Who is the author of *The Ghost with the Halloween Hiccups*? _____

5. What are the guide words on the encyclopedia page where "Halloween" is found? _____

6. Who is the publisher of *Arthur's Halloween*? _____

7. What are the guide words in the dictionary on the page where the word "pumpkin" is found? _____

8. On what page in the encyclopedia is the entry for "ghosts"? _____ In which volume is this entry? _____

HURRAY YOU'RE HERE!

THE PUMPKIN PATCH

© 1989 by The Center for Applied Research in Education

Name _____ Grade _____

BEAT THE WITCH TO THE PUMPKIN PATCH! II

The witch took 30 minutes to get to the pumpkin patch. Can you beat her by finding all the answers in less than 30 minutes?

START HERE!

1. How big was the biggest pumpkin ever grown? _____

2. On which day in the week will Halloween fall in the year 2000? _____

3. What is a wraith? _____

4. Houdini, the famous magician, died on Halloween. In what year did he die? _____

5. Edgar Allan Poe, a famous author, wrote many frightening stories. Where and when was he born?

6. Where is Transylvania? _____

7. An October radio broadcast of *The War of the World* was directed by Orson Welles. It frightened many people. When was it broadcast? _____

8. Use the card catalog to find a book about Halloween. Write the title and author.
   Title: _____
   Author: _____

9. Use a thesaurus to find three synonyms for the word, "ghost". _____

THE PUMPKIN PATCH

Name _____

Grade _____

© 1989 by The Center for Applied Research in Education

D. Research Activities for Autumn

TEACHER'S PAGE FOR
"HALLOWEEN FUN WITH THE DICTIONARY"

GRADE LEVELS: Grade 3, Grade 4 if additional dictionary practice is needed, Grade 2 for able groups

The activity on this page is to provide added practice in using the dictionary. The students are to look up the underlined word in the sentences below the boxes. Then in the correspondingly numbered box they are to make the illustration asked for in the sentence and also put the guide words from the dictionary page where they found the word in the blank spaces at the top of the box.

Provide each student with an activity sheet and a dictionary—one per child if possible, if not one per two students. Read the directions with the class and then ask if there are any questions. You may wish to do the first box of each activity. In this, as in any activity where students are working independently, all students will not finish at the same time, so be sure to have an additional activity ready for those who finish quickly. You could say that when the activity is finished, the students are to use the back of the paper to draw a picture of how they would like to dress up on Halloween. Another suggestion would be to have them make up a sentence or paragraph using all of the words which they have just looked up.

If the activity is done in the media center or library, it is helpful to provide crayons at each table since some students like to make their drawings more attractive and colorful.

At the end of the period or in the next class period, have the students take turns explaining the meaning of each word and the guide words where the word was found. Let those who wish show their illustrations, read their sentences, or show their Halloween picture.

KEY TO *HALLOWEEN FUN WITH THE DICTIONARY*:
(All guide words will vary depending on the dictionary used.) 1. A tiny jack o'lantern should be drawn 2. A huge jack o'lantern 3. An old woman or witch holding a black bag 4. Three owls 5. A very sad witch should be drawn 6. A very happy jack o'lantern should be pictured.

NOTES:

HALLOWEEN FUN WITH THE DICTIONARY!

Use a dictionary to help you follow the directions below. Look up the underlined word, follow the directions, and then put the guide words in the spaces in each box.

1. _____ _____   2. _____ _____   3. _____ _____

4. _____ _____   5. _____ _____   6. _____ _____

1. In box 1 make a *lilliputian* jack o'lantern.
2. In box 2 make a *gargantuan* jack o'lantern.
3. In box 3 make a *crone* holding a black bag.
4. In box 4 make a *triad* of owls.
5. In box 5 make a *melancholy* witch.
6. In box 6 make an *ecstatic* jack o'lantern!

Name _____ **Grade** _____

© 1989 by The Center for Applied Research in Education

D. Research Activities for Autumn

TEACHER'S PAGE FOR
"A PUZZLE FOR VETERAN'S DAY"

GRADE LEVELS: 5–8 (some 4th Grade groups)
SKILLS USED: Following directions, Research in Encyclopedia and Almanac

This activity might be used either prior to or after Veteran's Day. Most of the answers can be found in the almanac, although some, such as the first one, are more easily found in the encyclopedia.

Read the directions with the students. Academically able students should then be able to do the activities without any additional help. Other classes may need help to understand how to do the grid. It would help them to do the first question together. Ask the class which reference book is needed. When the response is the "V" volume of the encyclopedia, give as many "V" volumes of the encyclopedia to the students as possible. Have them look up Veteran's Day to tell the rest of the class the answer. When the first student has found the answer, Armistice Day, show the class how to first write Armistice Day in the blank spaces after the question and then how to cross off the letters of that answer in row one of the grid. Explain that when all the answers are crossed off in the grid, the remaining letters will spell a message.

Assign students to different questions if there will be a shortage of any particular reference book. Remind them that they are to do all of the questions and not just the one they begin on.

This activity could also be a contest or bonus activity in the Media Center or classroom.

KEY:

1.	A I R M I N S T N I C O E D A V Y E	1. Armistice Day
2.	M W O B R L E D W A R R W O N E E H	2. World War One
3.	O T H N E P R O E S R I D E O N T U	3. The President
4.	T H R E C O A V S T G E U A T R E D	4. The Coast Guard
5.	R S A A N T S U R ■ V E D T A Y E R	5. Saturday
6.	E A I S E N N S D H O A Y W I E S R	6. Eisenhower
7.	A U L Y L E S S G E S G R A A N L Y	7. Ulysses Grant
8.	H C O I V L I I L D A Y W I A N R A	8. Civil War
9.	L J I L O M M F Y C A T R H T E E R	9. Jimmy Carter
10.	F A I N F N A T Y P S O T L A I T S	10. Annapolis
11.	E W S E O S F T T P H Q E I U N N T	11. West Point
12.	I T A E D D M S I T R A A T L E S ■	12. Admiral

THE MESSAGE IS: In November we honor our veterans. Veteran's Day is a legal holiday in all of the 50 states of the United States.

A PUZZLE FOR VETERAN'S DAY

Veteran's Day was created as a day for citizens in our country to remember and honor the people in our Armed Forces. The Armed Forces protect our country and keep it safe.

Answer the following questions about Veteran's Day and the armed forces. Then cross off your answers in the grid. The remaining letters will spell a message. (A filled-in space represents a period.)

1. What was the original name for Veteran's Day?_____
2. After which war was this holiday begun?_____ _____ _____
3. Who is the head of all the armed forces?_____ _____
4. Which of the armed forces protects our coastline?_____ _____ _____
5. On what day of the week will Veteran's Day fall in the year 2000? (Veteran's Day is usually on November 11th.)_____
6. Our 34th President was a famous general. What is his last name?_____
7. Our 18th President was also a general? What was his name?_____ _____
8. In which war did he become famous?_____ _____
9. Our 39th president was once an officer in the navy? Who is he?_____ _____
10. Each of the armed forces has an academy where they train their officers. Where is the Naval Academy?_____
11. Where is the United States Military Academy?_____ _____
12. A general is the highest rank in the army. What is the highest rank an officer can attain in the navy?_____

THE MESSAGE IS:

_____
_____
_____
_____
_____
_____
_____
_____
_____
_____
_____
_____

1.	A	I	R	M	I	N	S	T	N	I	C	O	E	D	A	V	Y	E
2.	M	W	O	B	R	L	E	D	W	A	R	R	W	O	N	E	E	H
3.	O	T	H	N	E	P	R	O	E	S	R	I	D	E	O	N	T	U
4.	T	H	R	E	C	O	A	V	S	T	G	E	U	A	T	R	E	D
5.	R	S	A	A	N	T	S	U	R	■	V	E	D	T	A	Y	E	R
6.	E	A	I	S	E	N	N	S	D	H	O	A	Y	W	I	E	S	R
7.	A	U	L	Y	L	E	S	S	G	E	S	G	R	A	A	N	L	T
8.	H	C	O	I	V	L	I	I	L	D	A	Y	W	I	A	N	R	A
9.	L	J	I	L	O	M	M	F	Y	C	A	T	R	H	T	E	E	R
10.	F	A	I	N	F	N	A	T	Y	P	S	O	T	L	A	I	T	S
11.	E	W	S	E	O	S	F	T	T	P	H	O	E	I	U	N	N	T
12.	I	T	A	E	D	D	M	S	I	T	R	A	A	T	L	E	S	■

Name_____ Grade_____

D. Research Activities for Autumn

TEACHER'S PAGE FOR
"WHO IS THIS CHARACTER? A NATIONAL CHILDREN'S BOOK WEEK ACTIVITY"

GRADE LEVELS: Kindergarten–Grade 6

Each November National Children's Book Week is celebrated in most libraries and schools. Even though the week is usually squeezed in between Veteran's Day and Thanksgiving, take time to do some activity with your classes whether in the library/media center or the classroom.

Having the children make "Who is this Character?" posters to display during National Children's Book Week is fun.

To introduce the children to the activity show them the sample "WHO IS THIS CHARACTER?" poster of Peter Rabbit. It is a good idea to copy the page, color the character with felt tip pens or crayons, and mount it on colored paper before you show it to the class. First ask the children to guess who the character could be before you read them the information below the illustration. After letting the children guess different rabbit characters, read them the information below the poster. Most children will then know who the character is. Explain that they are to draw a favorite book character and then they are to fill in the information below the illustration. Tell them not to put the name of the character on their poster, but rather to write it on the back of the page. Hand out the blank posters and let the children begin. Crayons or felt-tip pens should be available to make the posters more attractive. At the end of the session or in the next class period, let each child show their poster, read their information, and let the class guess who the character is. Another way to use the posters would be to mount them on colored paper and put them on a bulletin board. Children could then guess who each character is. You could also provide answer sheets, number each poster, and have a contest to see which child can guess the most characters.

NOTES:

WHO IS THIS CHARACTER?

DESCRIPTION: He has white fur and long ears. Often seen wearing a blue coat with brass buttons.

PLACE OF RESIDENCE: He lives under a tree with his mother and three sisters.

FAVORITE ACTIVITIES: Going where he is not supposed to go to pick vegetables to eat.

FRIENDS: Likes to play with his sisters and occasionally talks to mice.

LAST SEEN: Hiding under a flowerpot in Mr. McGregor's garden.

© 1989 by The Center for Applied Research in Education

WHO IS THIS CHARACTER?

DESCRIPTION:_____

_____

_____

PLACE OF RESIDENCE:_____

_____

FAVORITE ACTIVITIES:_____

FRIENDS:_____

LAST SEEN:_____

_____

Name_____ **Grade**_____

© 1989 by The Center for Applied Research in Education

TEACHER'S PAGE FOR
"THAT'S THE PERFECT BOOK FOR YOU"

GRADE LEVELS: 4–6 (This may be more appropriate for top groups in Grade 4 since it is difficult.)
SKILLS: Thinking skills, Appreciation of Literature

This activity would be good to use during National Children's Book Week in November. It would also be appropriate for use during National Library Week in April.

It could be used as a Media Center contest during the week of Book Week or it could be used in a class situation.

The activity could be introduced by saying, "Which book do you think would be best for Goldilocks—a book about ships or a book on good manners?"

After the children answer this simple question and give their reason for their answer, you may wish to give them a few more characters and book titles before giving them the activity sheet. Other characters and books you might use could be: "Which book do you think would be the one Tom Sawyer would most enjoy—a book about the pirate Jean Lafitte or a book on car repair?" (If they should answer "car repair," remind them that cars were unheard of when Tom was a boy.)

You could also ask them which book Rapunzel might like best—a book on jogging or a book on hair care?

If the activity is to be used as a Media Center contest, post the students' imaginary or real titles which they assigned to the characters Arthur and Strega Nona at the bottom of the activity. In a class situation let each student who wishes to do so, read his titles for the characters.

> KEY:
> 1–I, 2–A, 3–K, 4–J, 5–M, 6–L, 7–O, 8–B,
> 9–G, 10–H, 11–C, 12–E, 13–F, 14–N, 15–D

THAT'S THE PERFECT BOOK FOR YOU!

Sometimes we read a book because we want to learn something. We might read a book to help us learn to draw, to build paper airplanes, or to do magic tricks.

Below are some fictional characters and some books they might want to check out. Match each character to the book which would be best for them.

1. The Great Brain _____
2. Curious George _____
3. The Three Little Pigs _____
4. Dorothy from *The Wizard of Oz* _____
5. Soup _____
6. Henry Huggins _____
7. Fudge _____
8. Mr. Popper _____
9. Danny Dunn _____
10. Encyclopedia Brown _____
11. Ellen Tebbitts _____
12. Mrs. Piggle Wiggle _____
13. Winnie The Pooh _____
14. Miss Nelson _____
15. Alice-in-Wonderland _____

A. A book titled *Everything You Want to Know About Everything*
B. A book about penguins and how they live
C. *The Complete Book of Ballet Dancing*
D. *The Care and Training of White Rabbits*
E. *The Complete Medical Book*
F. *One Hundred Ways to Use Honey*
G. A book on how to be an inventor
H. A book about Sherlock Holmes
I. A biography of Albert Einstein
J. A road atlas
K. *The Complete Book of Housebuilding*
L. A book on dog training
M. A book on how to win friends and influence people
N. A book on class management
O. A book on the care of turtles

No see if you can think of a book title (a real one or one you made up for these two characters).
Arthur (The Arthur books by Marc Brown) _____
Strega Nona (from books by Tomie De Paola) _____

Name_____ Grade_____

© 1989 by The Center for Applied Research in Education

TEACHER'S PAGE FOR "THANKSGIVING ART AND RESEARCH"

GRADE LEVELS: Grade 3, Grade 4 for added practice, and Grade 2 for able students

If you have used the preceding HALLOWEEN FUN WITH THE DICTIONARY with your class, the students will already know how to do the activity. If not explain the activity to the class. Be sure there are enough dictionaries so that no more than two have to share one. It is best, of course, if there are enough dictionaries so that each may have one. It is good to be sure that crayons are available for those who wish to illustrate the sentences in color.

Remind the students of the direction at the bottom of the page which tells them to "Make a festive November scene." Sometimes students will not notice the added direction. If there is time challenge the students to think up a sentence using all of the words they have just looked up.

Provide time at the close of the session or in the next class so that students can explain each word, list the guide words, and show their illustrations if they wish. Also give them time to show their festive November scene and read any sentences they may have written with the words.

> KEY:
> 1. A strong, heavy-looking Indian should be drawn.
> 2. A fat Pilgrim should be illustrated.
> 3. Food for the Thanksgiving dinner should be depicted.
> 4. A ship should be illustrated.
>
> On the back of the paper a happy, holiday-type scene should be drawn.

NOTES:

THANKSGIVING ART AND RESEARCH

Use the dictionary to help you decide what to draw in each box below. Put the guide words from the page where you found the underlined word in each box. When you are finished color each picture if there is time.

1. _____ _____

Make a *burly* Indian in this box.

2. _____ _____

Make a corpulent Pilgrim in this box.

3. _____ _____

Make a Thanksgiving *collation* in this box.

4. _____ _____

Make the Pilgrim's galleon in this box.

5. ON THE BACK OF THIS PAPER MAKE A FESTIVE NOVEMBER SCENE.

Name _____ **Grade** _____

UNIT II
Winter Activities

Activity

A. WINTER READING BINGOS
Directions for Winter Reading Bingos

ONCE-UPON-A-TIME READING BINGO
Teacher Directions
Student Bingo Card
Bulletin Board Squares
Certificates

FAVORITE AUTHORS READING BINGO
Teacher Directions
Student Bingo Card
Bulletin Board Squares
Bookmarks and Notes from Home
Certificates

B. WINTER STUDENT DETECTIVE ACTIVITIES

THE STUDENT DETECTIVE WINS A HOLIDAY BIKE
Teacher Directions and Key
Student Activity Page
Certificates

THE STUDENT DETECTIVE AND THE CASE OF THE MYSTERY WINTER VACATION
Teacher Directions and Key
Student Activity Page
Certificates

Skills Used

Reading Appreciation

Research in Card Catalog, Book of Quotations, Almanac, Encyclopedia

Research in Atlas

Activity	Skills Used

C. WINTER CROSSWORD COUNT PUZZLES
  Directions for Winter Crossword Counts
  Record of Scores for Winter Crossword Count Puzzles
	Dictionary and Thinking Skills

FUN IN THE SNOW CROSSWORD COUNT
  Student Activity Page
  Certificates	

CUPID—A VALENTINE CROSSWORD COUNT
  Student Activity Page
  Certificates	

LUCK OF THE IRISH CROSSWORD COUNT
  Student Activity Page
  Certificates	

D. FUN WITH FAIRYTALES Teacher Directions and Suggestions	

WANTED...
  Teacher Directions and Key
  Student Activity Page
	Reading Appreciation and Thinking Skills

FAIRYTALE ELEMENTS FOR CREATIVE WRITING
  Teacher Directions
  Reproducible Page
  Creative Writing Student Page
	Creative Writing and Thinking Skills

A MYSTERY MESSAGE FOR FAIRYTALE EXPERTS
  Teacher Directions and Key
  Student Activity Page
	Reading Appreciation and Thinking Skills

FAIRYTALE ACTIVITIES
  Teacher Directions
  Student Page
	Thinking Skills, Reading Appreciation, Creative Writing

E. RESEARCH ACTIVITIES FOR WINTER
  HOLIDAY BOOK SCRAMBLE
  Teacher Directions and Key
  Student Activity Page
	Reading Appreciation and Thinking Skills

Winter Activities

Activity	*Skills Used*
HOLIDAY RESEARCH A & B Teacher Directions and Keys Student Activity Page for A Student Activity Page for B	(A) Card Catalog and Dictionary (B) Book of Quotations, *Famous First Facts,* Encyclopedia, Card Catalog, *Guinness Book of World Records*
WHO SAID IT? Teacher Directions and Key Student Activity Page	Book of Quotations
DECEMBER DICTIONARY FUN Teacher Directions and Key Student Activity Page	Dictionary
HAPPY NEW YEAR Teacher Directions and Key Student Activity Page	Almanac
THE CHINESE ZODIAC Teacher Directions Student Activity Page	Encyclopedia, Creative Writing
VALENTINES FOR FAMOUS PEOPLE Teacher Directions and Key Student Activity Page	Almanac, Card Catalog, Encyclopedia
GREEN IS FOR THE IRISH Teacher Directions Shamrocks for Card Catalog Usage Blank Shamrock Page	Card Catalog and Shelving
A ST. PATRICK'S DAY JOURNEY Teacher Directions and Key Student Activity Page	Dewey Decimal Research
HELP THE LEPRECHAUN FIND THE POT OF GOLD Teacher Directions and Key Student Activity Page	Almanac, Encyclopedia

A. Winter Reading Bingos

DIRECTIONS FOR WINTER READING BINGOS

The winter bingos can be used at any time but because several famous fairytale/fantasy authors or compilers (Jakob Grimm, Charles Perrault, J.R. Tolkien, A.A. Milne, Michael Bond, Hugh Lofting, Bill Peet, Lloyd Alexander) were born in January, it is appropriate to use the "Once-Upon-a-Time" bingo at this time. The "Favorite Authors" bingo is fun to use at Valentine's Day because of the "love an author" and heart motif. It would also be good to use during either National Children's Book Week or National Library Week. The general directions on how to use the bingos are printed with the Autumn Bingos. Refer to those directions if you have not used the bingos before.

DIRECTIONS FOR "ONCE-UPON-A-TIME READING BINGO"

This bingo would be good to use in conjunction with a fairytale/fantasy unit. It could be featured in the entire media center/library as well as with individual classes. There are some activities in this winter unit to use with a fairytale/fantasy unit. Other things which could be done are to feature fantasy and fairytale books in the bulletin boards and displays in the media center. Fairytale and fantasy books could be read during the storytimes and featured in book talks to older students. The bingo bulletin board display itself will serve to focus attention on fairytale and fantasy books.

Once the bingo has begun and children begin bringing notes that they have read the specified books, the bingo sheets could be marked with a rubber stamp or sticker of a rainbow, butterfly, or unicorn.

Be sure to recognize the students who bingo by posting their name or pictures somewhere in the library or media center. This is gratifying to the winners and encourages others to participate. Prizes for the students who bingo by reading five books in any straight line could be an invitation to see a fairytale or fantasy movie or video in the media center. The movie could be anything from short fairytales for the younger children to a full-length movie for the older students. Another prize could be an invitation to an ice cream or popcorn party in the media center/library. Often members of the P.T.A. are willing to help with something like this. A balloon launch with all who bingo being allowed to put their name, address, and a message in a helium-filled balloon, which will be released at the end of the bingo, is also appropriate for this bingo.

The number of each bingo square to enlarge or duplicate for your bulletin board is as follows:

 4 of "YOUR CHOICE OF A FANTASY"
 3 each of "A BOOK OF FAIRYTALES," "AN ANIMAL FANTASY," "A *NARNIA* BOOK BY C. S. LEWIS"
 2 each of "A BOOK OF MYTHS," "TALL TALES," "AESOP'S FABLES," "A BOOK ABOUT ROBIN HOOD," "A CLASSIC FANTASY," and "A MODERN FANTASY."

If children need some suggestions for the various categories the following are but just a few of the many titles which would be appropriate:

AN ANIMAL FANTASY:

 For younger children any book by Burchard such as *Mother West Wind's "How" Stories*, E. B. White's *Charolotte's Web,* or for beginning readers any of the many books in the easy section in which animals can talk. For older students George Seldon's *Cricket in Times Square* and other animal fantasies or Robert Lawson's *Rabbit Hill* or Kenneth Graham's *Wind in the Willows* are but some of the many animal fantasies available.

A CLASSIC FANTASY:

 L. Frank Baum's *Wizard of Oz,* Collodi's *Pinocchio,* Lewis Carroll's *Alice in Wonderland,* Jonathan Swift's *Gulliver's Travels* are some of the classics available. A.A. Milne's *Winnie-the-Pooh* stories are appropriate for all grade levels and *Charlotte's Web* and the Paddington stories by Michael Bond are quickly becoming classics for the younger readers.

MODERN FANTASY:

 A Wrinkle in Time by Madeleine L'Engle (and most of her other books), *The Black Cauldron* by Lloyd Alexander, *The Crown* by Robin McKinley are but a few of the many fantasies written by modern authors.

ONCE-UPON-A-TIME READING BINGO

MYTHS FOLKTALES FANTASY FABLES FAIRYTALES

A BOOK OF FAIRYTALES	AN ANIMAL FANTASY	TALL TALES	AESOP'S FABLES	YOUR CHOICE OF A FANTASY
A BOOK ABOUT ROBIN HOOD	A CLASSIC FANTASY	A "NARNIA" BOOK BY C.S. LEWIS	A BOOK OF MYTHS	A MODERN FANTASY
AN ANIMAL FANTASY	A BOOK OF FAIRYTALES	A MODERN FANTASY	YOUR CHOICE OF A FANTASY	A BOOK OF MYTHS
TALL TALES	AESOP'S FABLES	YOUR CHOICE OF A FANTASY	A BOOK ABOUT ROBIN HOOD	A "NARNIA" BOOK BY C.S. LEWIS
A "NARNIA" BOOK BY C.S. LEWIS	YOUR CHOICE OF A FANTASY	A CLASSIC FANTASY	A BOOK OF FAIRYTALES	AN ANIMAL FANTASY

Record the title of each book you have read in the appropriate square or on the back of this page.

Name_____ Grade_____

© 1989 by The Center for Applied Research in Education

A Book Of Fairytales

An Animal Fantasy

© 1989 by The Center for Applied Research in Education

Your Choice of a Fantasy

A Book About Robin Hood

Tall Tales

Aesop's Fables

© 1989 by The Center for Applied Research in Education

A Classic Fantasy

A "Narnia" Book By C.S. Lewis

A Book of Myths

A Modern Fantasy

JOHN CHRISTOPHER
MADELEINE L'ENGLE
ANDRE NORTON
LYNN REID BANKS
ROBIN McKINLEY

© 1989 by The Center for Applied Research in Education

© 1989 by The Center for Applied Research in Education

FUN WITH FANTASY

IT'S NO LIE! I LOVE A FANTASY

THERE IS MAGIC IN A FAIRYTALE!

READ A TALL TALE

NOTE FROM HOME	NOTE FROM HOME
_____	_____
(Child's Name)	(Child's Name)
HAS READ THE BOOK:	HAS READ THE BOOK:
_____	_____
FOR THE ONCE-UPON-A-TIME READING BINGO	FOR THE ONCE-UPON-A-TIME READING BINGO
....	....
(SIGNATURE OF PARENT OR ANOTHER RESPONSIBLE ADULT)	(SIGNATURE OF PARENT OR ANOTHER RESPONSIBLE ADULT)

THIS CERTIFIES THAT

HAS COMPLETED A BINGO IN THE

Once Upon-A-Time Reading Bingo

Signature of teacher or librarian

THIS CERTIFIES THAT

HAS COMPLETED A BINGO IN THE

Once Upon-A-Time Reading Bingo

Signature of teacher or librarian

© 1989 by The Center for Applied Research in Education

A. Winter Reading Bingos

DIRECTIONS FOR "FAVORITE AUTHORS READING BINGO"

This bingo is prepared in a different way from the previous bingos because there are far too many favorite authors to limit to ten categories. There is also a need to have a bingo for beginning readers as well as the older students, so for this reason there are two bingos—one for older readers and one for younger readers.

For this bingo copy or enlarge the heart patterns to make 25 hearts. These hearts can be mounted all on the same color square, or alternately use a different color—such as pink alternated with white and mounted on a red background. After the 25 squares are prepared, mount them on the bulletin board in a bingo board pattern. Then enlarge or copy the author's names and mount them on the hearts in the exact pattern of the student bingo sheets. Since there are two bingo sheets and two sets of authors' names, you can either prepare two separate bulletin boards or mount both sets of authors' names on the same bulletin board. To distinguish which authors are meant for younger readers, the names could be on different colors—i.e., the authors for younger students outlined in red ink and the authors for older students outlined in black. Be sure that the authors' names are in the same order as the students' bingo cards. Using this method, the first heart would have both the names of Donald Sobol (for the older student's bingo) and Marc Brown (for younger or less-qualified readers).

If you think the students in your school have other favorite authors, you could change the bingo sheet and the bulletin board. There was no way to include all of the authors, but these authors are some of the favorites of children and not necessarily authors who will win a Newberry or Caldecott award.

After mounting the squares in the bingo pattern, make large letters or use pin-back plastic letters to spell out the title of the bingo above the squares.

Once the sample bingo card bulletin board is prepared, follow the same procedure to play the bingo as in the previous games.

Activities which might be fun and fit in with this bingo would be to have each class vote for their favorite author. When the author is chosen they could prepare a large heart or valentine with that author's name on it and mount the heart or valentine on their classroom door. Some of the classes might want to write to their elected author either individually or as a class.

A school-wide vote for the school's favorite author would also be fun. After an author is chosen, his/her books could be featured. It would be interesting to keep a tally to see how many books by the author were read during the school year. A letter to the author could be written to let the author know of his/her selection by your school.

To mark the bingo cards for the students, a heart made with a rubber stamp or a valentine sticker could be used.

Be sure to post the names of the students who bingo or take their picture and post it.

During the bingo, or as a culmination activity, it would be nice to have an author visit the school and talk to the students. This activity should be for the entire school, but, if used as a culminating activity, bingo winners could perhaps have lunch with the author or receive a paperback book autographed by the author. P.T.A. groups will often furnish the money required to have an author visit.

If it is not possible to have an author visit, a "favorite author" party could be held in the media center or library where the students could be given a treat and see either a movie or hear a storyteller.

Favorite Authors Reading Bingo

DONALD SOBOL	YOUR CHOICE FICTION	BEVERLY CLEARLY	LAURA INGALLS WILDER	JUDY BLUME
ROBERT PECK	ELLEN CONFORD	YOUR CHOICE NON-FICTION	YOUR CHOICE FICTION	BETSY BYARS
YOUR CHOICE FICTION	WALT MOREY	JOHN FITZGERALD	BARBARA PARK	LOIS LOWRY
CONSTANCE GREENE	YOUR CHOICE NON-FICTION	ZILPHA SNYDER	PATRICIA REILLY GIFF	YOUR CHOICE FICTION
JAMIE GILSON	FLORENCE PARRY HEIDE	LYNN REID BANKS	BETTY REN WRIGHT	YOUR CHOICE NON-FICTION

MY FAVORITE AUTHOR IS: _____

Name _____   **Grade** _____

© 1989 by The Center for Applied Research in Education

DONALD SOBOL	YOUR CHOICE–FICTION
BEVERLY CLEARY	LAURA INGALLS WILDER
JUDY BLUME	ROBERT PECK
ELLEN CONFORD	YOUR CHOICE–NON-FICTION
BETSY BYARS	WALT MOREY

© 1989 by The Center for Applied Research in Education

JOHN FITZGERALD	BARBARA PARK
LOIS LOWRY	CONSTANCE GREENE
ZILPHA SNYDER	PATRICIA REILLY GIFF
JAMIE GILSON	FLORENCE PARRY HEIDE
LYNN REID BANKS	BETTY REN WRIGHT

© 1989 by The Center for Applied Research in Education

Favorite Authors Reading Bingo (Primary)

MARC BROWN	YOUR CHOICE FICTION	DR. SEUSS	H.A. REY	HARRY ALLARD
MERCER MAYER	JAMES MARSHALL	YOUR CHOICE NON-FICTION	YOUR CHOICE FICTION	CHRIS VAN ALLSBURG
YOUR CHOICE FICTION	JUDY BLUME	BETSY HAYWOOD	GERTRUDE WARNER	RUTH CHEW
DONALD SOBOL	YOUR CHOICE NON-FICTION	E. B. WHITE	LAURA INGALLS WILDER	E. W. HILDICK
FLORENCE PARRY HEIDE	PATRICIA REILLY GIFF	BEVERLY CLEARY	YOUR CHOICE NON-FICTION	YOUR CHOICE FICTION

Record the titles of the books you have read in the appropriate square or on the back of this page.

MY FAVORITE AUTHOR IS: _____

Name _____ Grade _____

© 1989 by The Center for Applied Research in Education

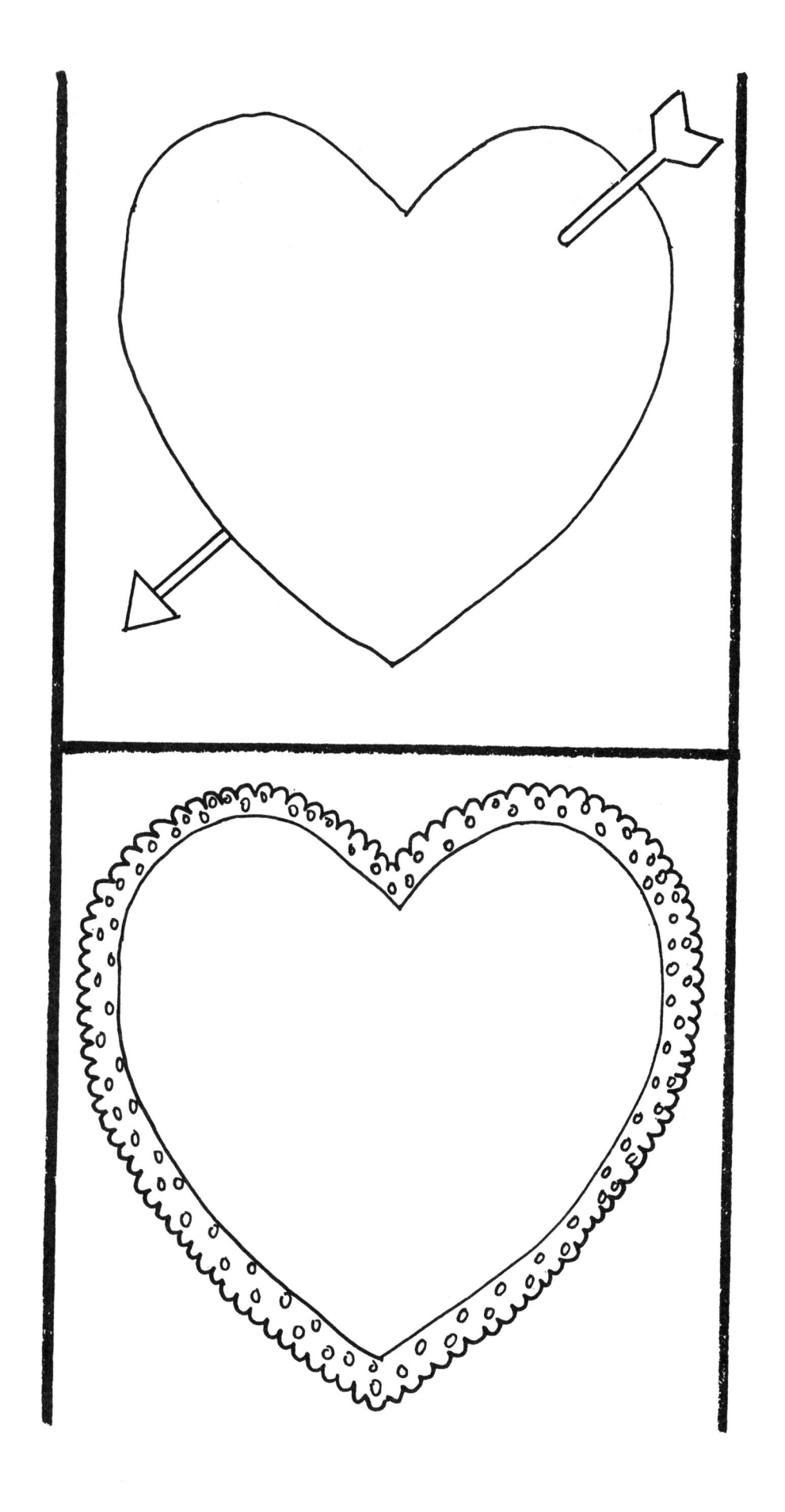

© 1989 by The Center for Applied Research in Education

MARC BROWN	YOUR CHOICE–FICTION
MERCER MAYER	JAMES MARSHALL
YOUR CHOICE–NON-FICTION	CHRIS VAN ALLSBURG
JUDY BLUME	BETSY HAYWOOD
GERTRUDE WARNER	RUTH CHEW

DONALD SOBOL	E. B. WHITE
LAURA INGALLS WILDER	E. W. HILDICK
FLORENCE PARRY HEIDE	PATRICIA REILLY GIFF
BEVERLY CLEARY	DR. SEUSS
H. A. REY	HARRY ALLARD

My Favorite Authors Are:

_____
_____
_____
_____
_____
_____
_____
_____

♥ ♥ ♥ ♥

HAVE YOU READ A BOOK BY THESE FAVORITE AUTHORS?

JUDY BLUME
JAMIE GILSON
BEVERLY CLEARY
DONALD SOBOL
JOHN CHRISTOPHER
BETSY BYARS
JOHN FITZGERALD
PATRICIA GIFF
ELLEN CONFORD

I LOVE BOOKS BY MY FAVORITE AUTHOR!

MY FAVORITE AUTHOR IS: _____

READ A BOOK BY ONE OF THESE AUTHORS!

- MARC BROWN
- DR. SEUSS
- MERCER MAYER
- Harry ALLARD
- STEVEN KELLOG
- ERIC CARLE

NOTE FROM HOME

_____
(Child's Name)
HAS READ THE BOOK:

_____

FOR THE

_____
(SIGNATURE OF PARENT OR ANOTHER RESPONSIBLE ADULT)

I LOVE BOOKS

NOTE FROM HOME

_____
(Child's Name)
HAS READ THE BOOK:

_____

FOR THE

_____
(SIGNATURE OF PARENT OR ANOTHER RESPONSIBLE ADULT)

© 1989 by The Center for Applied Research in Education

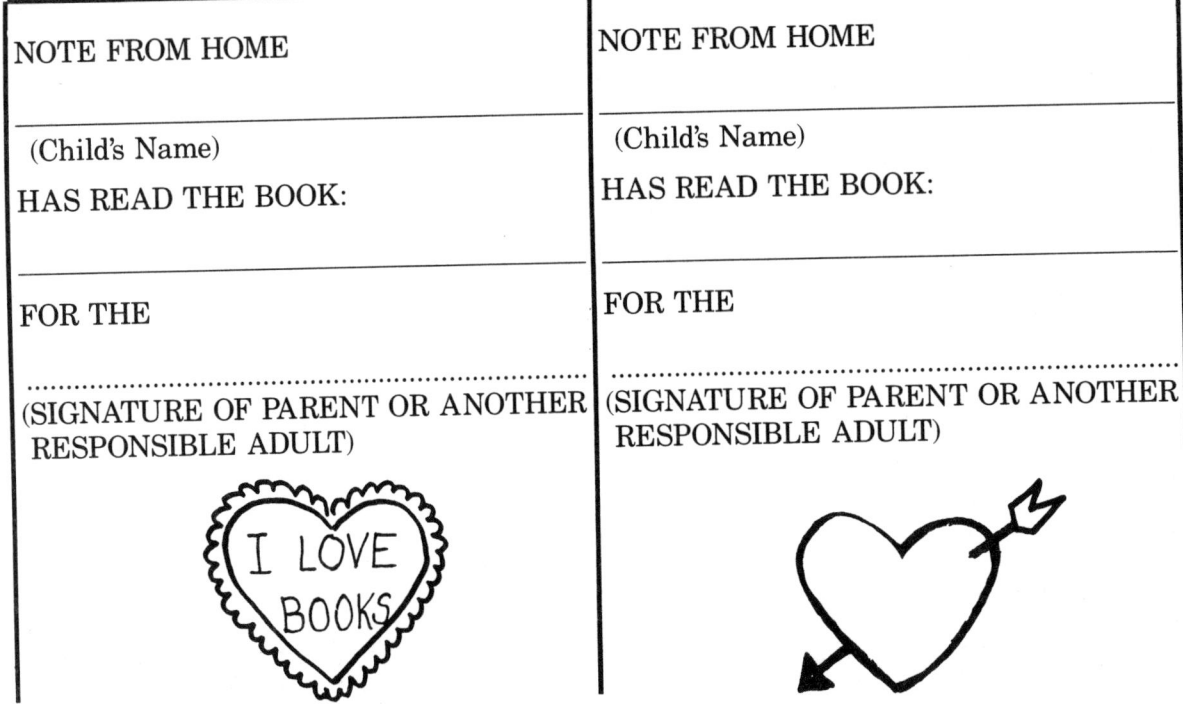

THIS CERTIFIES THAT

HAS COMPLETED A BINGO IN THE

Favorite Authors Reading Bingo

Signature of teacher or librarian

© 1989 by The Center for Applied Research in Education

THIS CERTIFIES THAT

HAS COMPLETED A BINGO IN THE

Favorite Authors Reading Bingo

Signature of teacher or librarian

B. Winter Student Detective Activities

TEACHER'S PAGE FOR
"THE STUDENT DETECTIVE WINS A HOLIDAY BIKE"

GRADE LEVELS: 5–8

This Student Detective activity involves the use of a book of quotations, the card catalog, the almanac, and a geographical dictionary. It can be used in any class familiar with the reference sources, but is probably most useful in grades five through eight.

Read the beginning paragraphs together as a class and explain that the answers are to be put after the clue and then the letter called for in the box below the clues. If the class is a capable or gifted class, let them proceed by themselves. If you think your class might need help determining the reference source for each question, go over the clues together and as a class decide which reference source is best. After doing this you might want to start different students on each question so that there will not be too big a demand for reference sources in which you are limited.

The activity can also be used as an extra media center/library activity with a prize and a certificate (provided in this book) awarded to each participant who successfully does the activity. Students who show an interest in doing this activity in their free time should be given any help they might need so that they will not be frustrated and will be successful, thereby discovering the fun of research.

> KEY AND SOURCES USED:
> 1. Henry Wadsworth Longfellow—*Bartlett's Familiar Quotations*
> 2. Theodore Taylor—Card Catalog
> 3. Arizona—*World Almanac*
> 4. Ulysses S. Grant—almanac or encyclopedia
> 5. Harry Allard—Card Catalog
> 6. Australia—Geographical Dictionary
> 7. Seoul, South Korea—*World Almanac*
> 8. Santa Fe, New Mexico—*World Almanac*
> 9. Eleanor Cameron—Card Catalog
> 10. Odgen Nash—*Barlett's Book of Famous Quotations*
> THE FAMOUS NAME IS: SANTA CLAUS.

Winter Student Detective Activities

NOTES:

THE STUDENT DETECTIVE WINS A HOLIDAY BIKE

The Student Detective looked at the poster on the wall of the store. The sign said, "KIDS! WIN A NEW BICYCLE FOR THE HOLIDAYS. BE THE FIRST TO FIGURE OUT THE NAME OF THIS FAMOUS PERSON AND YOU WILL WIN A BICYCLE OF YOUR CHOICE! GET THE CLUES IN OUR STORE!

"That sounds like fun!" said the Student Detective. She went into the store, got the clues, and then got busy. It took the Student Detective 40 minutes to solve the clues and win the holiday bicycle. Can you figure the clues out faster than the Student Detective? Try it and see! THE CLUES ARE BELOW. (Put the answer to each clue beside the clue and the letter called for in the blank spaces below the clues.) GOOD LUCK!

CLUE #1: The 7th letter of the famous name is the letter which begins the last name of the person who said, "And the song from beginning to end, I found in the heart of a friend."_____

CLUE #2: The 4th letter of the name is the same as the 1st letter of the last name of the author of *The Cay*._____

CLUE #3: The 5th letter of the name is the same as the *last* letter of the state which entered the Union on February 14, 1912._____

CLUE #4: The 9th letter of the name is the same as the 1st letter of the first name of our 18th president._____

CLUE #5: The 2nd letter of the name is the same as the 1st letter of the last name of the author of *Miss Nelson Is Missing*._____

CLUE #6. The 8th letter of the name is the same as the 1st letter of the country whose capital is Canberra._____

CLUE #7. The 1st letter of the name is the same as the 1st letter of the city where a disastrous fire occurred in a theatre on November 3, 1974._____

CLUE #8. The 10th letter is the same as the 1st letter of the state capital of the state who entered the Union on January 6, 1912._____

CLUE #9. The 6th letter is the same as the 1st letter of the last name of the author of *The Wonderful Flight to the Mushroom Planet*._____

CLUE #10: The 3rd letter is the same as the 1st letter of the last name of the person who said, "I think that I shall never see, a billboard lovely as a tree."_____

AND YOUR ANSWER IS: THE FAMOUS NAME IS:

___ ___ ___ ___ ___ ___ ___ ___ ___ ___
1.   2.   3.   4.   5.   6.   7.   8.   9.   10.

Name_____ **Grade**_____

© 1989 by The Center for Applied Research in Education

_____

is awarded the title of:

Super Student Detective

for solving the case of

THE STUDENT DETECTIVE WINS A HOLIDAY BIKE

_____
Signature of teacher or librarian

_____ (date)

_____

is awarded the title of:

Super Student Detective

for solving the case of

THE STUDENT DETECTIVE WINS A HOLIDAY BIKE

_____
Signature of teacher or librarian

_____ (date)

© 1989 by The Center for Applied Research in Education

TEACHER'S PAGE FOR
"THE STUDENT DETECTIVE AND THE CASE OF THE MYSTERY WINTER VACATION"

GRADE LEVELS: 4-6 (or any class which needs extra work with an atlas)

This activity could be used either before or after the winter vacation break. It could also be used as extra practice for working with the atlas and latitude and longitude. It, like other Student Detective activities, can also be used as an independent activity in the media center or library with a certificate and prize awarded to each successful participant.

If used in a class, read the opening paragraphs and the letter to the Student Detective together. Discuss which reference source is needed and then, depending on the ability level of the class, let the students do the work independently, or if needed find the first location together. Since most schools have a classroom-size set of atlases, there should be no problem with having enough reference sources for each student.

An extra activity for those who finish or for the entire class could be for each student to plan their dream vacation using latitude and longitude as directions. Let each student share their vacation spot's latitude and longitude with the class and see if the class can locate the place. This could be done in the next class period and would provide extra practice with the atlas.

KEY: (ALL ANSWERS ARE FOUND BY USING AN ATLAS*)
1. Bob started his vacation in *Salem, Oregon*. His first stop was *Denver, Colorado*. He then went to *Lincoln, Nebraska*. Then he went to *Indianapolis, Indiana*. He had fun in *Harrisburg, Pennsylvania*. His next stop was *Portland, Maine*. Then he went to the big city of *New York, New York*. His last stop was in the beautiful state of *Florida*.

NOTES:_____
_____
_____
_____
_____
_____

*Latitudes and longitudes are from *Oxford World Atlas* (1973)

THE STUDENT DETECTIVE AND THE CASE OF THE MYSTERY WINTER VACATION

Winter break was not much fun for the student detective because his best friend was gone on vacation. The Student Detective was bored for without his best friend he could think of nothing to do.

He was pleasantly surprised one day when a letter came from his friend. He opened it expecting to hear all about Bob's vacation. Instead Bob's letter gave him something to do. Here is the letter.

Dear Student D.,

I know how much you like to solve mysteries so I thought instead of telling you about all the places I've been to on my vacation, I would let you figure it out. I've written the approximate latitude and longitude of each place where I've visited. I'm sure you can figure out where each place is. I hope you have as much fun figuring out my travels as I have had going to each place.

Your friend,
Bob

P.S.: If you can't figure out where I've been, wait until I get home and I'll tell you all about it!

BOB'S TRIP

I started my vacation in a state capital with the latitude of 44°N, 123°W.

My first stop was in a state capital with an approximate lat. of 39°N, 105°W.

My next stop was a state capital with an approximate lat. of 40°N., 96°W.

I next went to the state capital with a latitude of 39°N, 86°W.

I had fun in the capital of a large state whose latitude was 40°N, long. 76°W.

My next stop sounded like I was near my home but it was really far away. Its latitude was 43°N, 70°W.

I then went to a large city with a latitude of 40°N and 73°W.

My last stop was in a beautiful state that is almost entirely between 25°-20°N. latitude and between 80°-85°W longitude.

THE STUDENT DETECTIVE HAD FUN FINDING OUT WHERE BOB HAD BEEN. Can you figure it out too. Put your answers in the spaces below:

Bob started his vacation in _____, _____. His first stop was _____, _____. He then went to _____, _____. Then he went to _____, _____. He then had fun in _____, _____. His next stop was _____, _____. Then he went to the big city of _____, _____. His last stop was in the beautiful state of _____.

Name_____ Grade_____

© 1989 by The Center for Applied Research in Education

_____

is awarded the title of

Super

Student Detective

for solving

THE CASE OF THE MYSTERY WINTER VACATION

_____
Signature of teacher or librarian

_____
(Date)

_____

is awarded the title of

Super

Student Detective

for solving

THE CASE OF THE MYSTERY WINTER VACATION

_____
Signature of teacher or librarian

_____
(Date)

© 1989 by The Center for Applied Research in Education

C. Winter Crossword Count Puzzles

DIRECTIONS FOR WINTER CROSSWORD COUNTS

The Winter Crossword Counts, like the Autumn ones, can be used in either a classroom situation or in the library/media center as a contest for individual participation.

If used in a library or media center, the highest score achieved at each grade level the year before could be posted and students could try to get a higher score. They should understand, however, that they need only be highest for their class for the current year in order to be declared a winner. If possible, all students who try the crossword count should be awarded a sticker or bookmark for trying since it is an individual choice rather than an assignment. Certificates are included which could be awarded to the highest and second highest scores at each grade level. Be sure to award certificates at each grade level for first and second graders should not be competing with fifth and sixth graders. At some time you may even want to have a staff contest with the staff competing to see who can find the words which will attain the highest score.

In the classroom situation, give each student a dictionary, if possible, and see who can find the highest point words in 20 or 25 minutes.

The first winter crossword contest, FUN IN THE SNOW, is like the Autumn puzzles in that words need be formed only horizontally. (You may wish to challenge able students to make their words also form words vertically.) Explain to the students that each letter has a point count and that they are to use a dictionary to try to find words with high point letters.

The CUPID VALENTINE Crossword Count is different only in that the word cupid is used as part of the two vertical words. The "C" is the first letter of the left vertical word and the "D" the first letter of the vertical word on the right of the square. The last letter of these two vertical words form the first and last letter of the horizontal word at the bottom of the square.

Following is a chart where you may keep a record of past winners. Students enjoy hearing these scores so it will probably be worthwhile to keep a record.

THE LUCK OF THE IRISH puzzle features the word, "leprechaun." Have the children form words horizontally only, unless you have a gifted or talented group who could also form words vertically.

RECORD OF SCORES FOR FUN IN THE SNOW CROSSWORD COUNT

YEAR	GRADE	SCORE	PERSON ACHIEVING THE SCORE

RECORD OF SCORES FOR CUPID VALENTINE CROSSWORD COUNT

YEAR	GRADE	SCORE	PERSON ACHIEVING THE SCORE

RECORD OF SCORES FOR LUCK OF THE IRISH CROSSWORD COUNT

YEAR	GRADE	SCORE	PERSON ACHIEVING THE SCORE

FUN IN THE SNOW CROSSWORD COUNT

See what a high point count you can get by getting out your dictionaries and trying to find words which have letters with high point counts. Do not use proper nouns. The words should go from left to right and do not need to go up and down. GOOD LUCK!

POINT COUNT OF LETTERS
- A = 21
- B = 7
- C = 20
- D = 19
- E = 18
- F = 17
- G = 16
- H = 15
- I = 14
- J = 13
- K = 12
- L = 11
- M = 22
- N = 25
- O = 24
- P = 10
- Q = 2
- R = 9
- S = 26
- T = 8
- U = 3
- V = 4
- W = 23
- X = 5
- Y = 6
- Z = 1

Box 1:____ Box 2:____ Box 3:____
Box 4:____ Box 5:____ Box 6:____
Box 7:____ Box 8:____ Box 9:____
Box 10:____ Box 11:____ Box 12:____
Box 13:____ Box 14:____ Box 15:____
Box 16:____ Box 17:____ Box 18:____

TOTAL:____

Name_____ Grade_____

© 1989 by The Center for Applied Research in Education

1st

HAS WON FIRST PLACE IN THE

Fun in the Snow

CROSSWORD COUNT CONTEST.

TEACHER/LIBRARIAN

DATE: _____

2nd

HAS WON SECOND PRIZE IN THE

Fun in the Snow

CROSSWORD COUNT CONTEST.

TEACHER/LIBRARIAN

DATE: _____

© 1989 by The Center for Applied Research in Education

CUPID
A VALENTINE CROSSWORD COUNT

See how many points you can get by filling in this crossword count puzzle. Each letter of the alphabet has a certain number of points. Try to use the letters with the most points. The letters of the words "Cupid's Arrows" have the most points. You may use any words you find in the dictionary except proper nouns. Please don't let Mom or Dad help you!

GOOD LUCK!

C	U	P	I	D
1.				2.
3.				4.
5.				6.
7.	8.	9.	10.	11.

LETTER POINT COUNT
- A: 20
- B: 16
- C: 26
- D: 22
- E: 15
- F: 14
- G: 13
- H: 12
- I: 23
- J: 11
- K: 10
- L: 9
- M: 8
- N: 7
- O: 18
- P: 24
- Q: 6
- R: 19
- S: 21
- T: 5
- U: 25
- V: 4
- W: 17
- X: 3
- Y: 2
- Z: 1

MY SCORE IS:

Box 1:_____ Box 2:_____ Box 3:_____

Box 4:_____ Box 5:_____ Box 6:_____

Box 7:_____ Box 8:_____ Box 9:_____

Box 10:_____ Box 11:_____

MY TOTAL SCORE IS:_____

Name_____ Grade_____

© 1989 by The Center for Applied Research in Education

_____
HAS WON FIRST PLACE IN THE

Cupid Valentine

CROSSWORD COUNT CONTEST.

_____
TEACHER/LIBRARIAN

DATE:_____

1st

_____
HAS WON SECOND PRIZE IN THE

Cupid Valentine

CROSSWORD COUNT CONTEST.

_____
TEACHER/LIBRARIAN

DATE:_____

2nd

© 1989 by The Center for Applied Research in Education

LUCK OF THE IRISH CROSSWORD COUNT

Fill in this Crossword count for March. The letters used in "Leprechaun" have the greatest value so try to use them often. Use a dictionary to help you but not Mom or Dad!

Put words in the puzzle horizontally (across) but you need not make the words go up and down (vertically).

See if you can have the highest score.

GOOD LUCK!

LETTER POINT VALUE:
A: 20
B: 17
C: 22
D: 16
E: 25
F: 15
G: 14
H: 21
I: 13
J: 12
K: 11
L: 26
M: 10
N: 18
O: 9
P: 24
Q: 8
R: 23
S: 6
T: 5
U: 19
V: 4
W: 7
X: 2
Y: 3
Z: 1

MY SCORE:

WORD "A": Box 1:___ Box 2:___ TOTAL:___

WORD "B": Box 3:___ Box 4:___ Box 5:___ Box 6:___ TOTAL:___

WORD "C": Box 7:___ Box 8:___ Box 9:___ Box 10:___ Box 11:___ Box 12:___ TOTAL:___

(Continued on next page)

WORD "D": Box 13:___ Box 14:___ Box 15:___ Box 16:___ Box 17:___ Box 18:___ Box 19:___

Box 20:___ TOTAL:___

WORD "E": Box 21:___ Box 22:___ Box 23:___ Box 24:___ Box 25:___ Box 26:___ Box 27:___

Box 28:___ TOTAL:___

WORD "F": Box 29:___ Box 30:___ Box 31:___ Box 32:___ Box 33:___ Box 34:___ TOTAL:___

WORD "G": Box 35:___ Box 36:___ Box 37:___ Box 38:___ TOTAL:___

WORD "H": Box 39:___ Box 40:___ TOTAL:___ TOTAL OF ALL WORDS:___

MY SCORE FROM ALL WORDS IS:_____.

Name_____ **Grade**_____

1st

_____
HAS WON FIRST PLACE IN THE

Luck of the Irish
CROSSWORD COUNT CONTEST.

_____
TEACHER/LIBRARIAN

DATE:_____

2nd

_____
HAS WON SECOND PRIZE IN THE

Luck of the Irish
CROSSWORD COUNT CONTEST.

_____
TEACHER/LIBRARIAN

DATE: _____

© 1989 by The Center for Applied Research in Education

D. Fun with Fairytales

TEACHER DIRECTIONS AND SUGGESTIONS

A fairytale unit is fun to do at any time of the year, but it is especially appropriate during the month of January since so many authors of fantasy and compilers of fairytales were born in that month. Some of these authors include Jacob Grimm—January 4, Charles Perrault—January 12, J. R. R. Tolkien—January 3, A. A. Milne—January 13, Hugh Lofting—January 14, and Lloyd Alexander—January 30.

A fairytale unit works well with children in grades three through five. Most children in grades four through five can do the material here, while some third graders can do most of it.

The unit could begin by showing several fairytales on video, film, or sound filmstrip. After the children have seen several, have them identify the common elements of a fairytale. Then whenever you show a fairytale or the children read one and report on it, have them identify the fairytale elements in the fairytale. Some of these elements are good wins out over evil; a poor boy or girl who gains riches; a king, queen, or other royal person; animals which can talk; a witch, fairy, or giant; the numbers three or seven; etc. Older students can keep a record of the fairytales they have read or seen and list the fairytale elements in each.

The activities which follow could be used as a culmination of a fairytale unit or in conjunction with the unit.

D. Fun with Fairytales

WANTED...
TEACHER DIRECTIONS

    This activity is usually fun for the children. If you feel the activity might be too easy for your group, read the wanted descriptions and let them respond orally rather than using the activity page. Then challenge them to make a "Wanted" poster of their own of some folk or fairytale character. (For those classes using the activity as a written assignment, the directions at the bottom of the page direct the student to make a "Wanted" poster on the back.)

    When the posters and descriptions are completed, let each student show his/her poster and read their descriptions. Let the class try to guess which character is "wanted." When the class is over, the "Wanted" posters could be put on a bulletin board for other students to see.

> KEY 1. JACK IN THE BEANSTALK 2. THE BIG BAD WOLF
>   3. GOLDILOCKS   4. ABDUHL GAZAZI (from *The Garden of Abduhl Gazazi* by Chris Van Allsburg)
>   5. The troll in THREE BILLY GOATS GRUFF
>   6. The Wolf in LITTLE RED RIDING HOOD

NOTES:_____

WANTED...

These fictional characters from old or new fairytales or folktales all did something they should not have done. If there were a "Wanted" poster for each of them, could you tell who each one was?

WRITE THE NAMES OF THE FICTIONAL CHARACTERS ON THE BLANK LINE AT THE BOTTOM OF EACH POSTER AND THEN DRAW A PICTURE OF THE CHARACTERS ABOVE THE NAME.

1. WANTED	2. WANTED	3. WANTED
For stealing a hen, a bag of gold, and a musical Instrument. Description: Male, young	For Vandalism. Destroyed two houses, attempted to destroy a third. Description: Dangerous. Large Teeth.	For entering a home while owners absent, breaking furniture, stealing food. Description: Blonde Female
4. WANTED	5. WANTED	6. WANTED
On suspicion of changing a dog into a duck. Description: once a magician, hates dogs, loves gardens.	For stopping traffic on a bridge. Hides under bridge and will not let anyone cross. Description: Has a Loud, Rough Voice.	For impersonating an elderly person and for telling lies to children. Description: Big Teeth, Big Eyes, and Big ears.

On the back of this paper see if you can make a wanted poster. Draw the character and write the description but do not add the name. See if the class can guess who your character is.

Name_____ Grade_____

© 1989 by The Center for Applied Research in Education

D. Fun with Fairytales

FAIRYTALE ELEMENTS FOR CREATIVE WRITING
TEACHER DIRECTIONS

Make a copy of the page "Fairytale Elements for Creative Writing." Mount the copy on tagboard or railroad board and then cut apart on dotted lines. (You may wish to laminate it first to insure longer life.) Put the cut-apart fairytale elements in a hat or box and let each child draw out one card containing three fairytale elements. Hand each child a copy of the page, "Once Upon a Time..."

Tell the class that they are to write their own fairytale, being sure to incorporate the three elements on the card which they have drawn. Make sure they understand that they are not limited to only these three elements, but the elements they have drawn must be included in their story.

If this activity is done after children have seen or read many fairytales, most children need little extra help to write the stories. If any child needs help, work with him or her individually picking out first a character and then seeing how the character could be used with the three elements he/she has drawn.

After the stories are written and illustrated, allow time, probably in the next session, to let each student read his/her fairytale. After each reading, have the class try to guess which fairytale elements the author had drawn and incorporated into the story. Another way would be for the author to first tell the class the elements he had drawn and then let the class listen to the story and determine if he/she had effectively used those elements.

NOTES:

FAIRYTALE ELEMENTS FOR CREATIVE WRITING

1. A castle 2. A poor son or daughter 3. A magic wand	1. A king or queen 2. A magic wand 3. A giant
1. The hour of midnight 2. The number three 3. A magic spell	1. A castle 2. A magic spell 3. A troll
1. A treasure found 2. A fairy godmother 3. Wish or wishes granted	1. The forest 2. The number seven 3. A magic happening
1. The youngest winning something 2. A giant 3. The number three	1. The number seven 2. A prince 3. A wicked stepmother
1. A magic spell 2. The number seven 3. The forest	1. The number three 2. A magic wand 3. A prince changed into an animal
1. A wish or wishes granted 2. Talking animals 3. The youngest winning something	1. Wish or wishes granted 2. A fairy or an elf 3. A giant
1. A fairy or elf 2. A prince or princess 3. A forest	1. Animals that can talk 2. A witch or a wizard 3. A king or queen
1. A troll 2. The number seven 3. A treasure found	1. A prince or princess 2. A poor boy or girl 3. The hour of midnight
1. A witch or a wizard 2. The number three 3. A giant	1. A castle 2. A treasure found 3. A witch or wizard

© 1989 by The Center for Applied Research in Education

By _____

Once upon a time _____

(If you need more room please use the back of this page.)

A MYSTERY MESSAGE FOR FAIRYTALE EXPERTS
TEACHER DIRECTIONS AND KEY

This activity should probably be a culminating activity used after the children have seen, heard, and read many fairytales. Pass out the activity sheet to the class and read the directions together. Do the first one together and show the class how they are to cross out their answer in the grid below the sentences. Explain that the remaining letters from all of the lines of the grid will spell out a message. Explain black spaces signify periods in the message.

If you have time or if there are some students who finish the work quickly, pass out graph paper and let the students try to make up their own "mystery message."

KEY:

1.	C	S	L	I	E	N	E	R	D	I	N	E	G	B	E	R	A	U	T	Y	E	SLEEPING BEAUTY
2.	L	C	L	I	A	N	H	D	A	E	D	R	A	E	B	L	L	A	A	L	L	CINDERELLA
3.	A	W	N	I	Z	D	A	Y	R	D	O	O	U	F	W	I	L	O	L	Z	T	WIZARD OF OZ
4.	O	O	P	I	I	F	N	Y	O	O	U	C	L	I	C	H	K	I	E	T	O	PINOCCHIO
5.	H	O	A	N	R	E	S	E	L	A	A	N	D	G	R	D	E	T	F	E	L	HANSEL & GRETEL
6.	A	S	I	N	R	O	Y	W	T	A	W	L	H	E	I	S	■	T	R	E	E	SNOW WHITE
7.	T	A	H	D	E	A	F	R	O	A	I	G	P	R	R	I	Y	N	C	E		THE FROG PRINCE
8.	R	T	A	U	S	L	S	I	N	E	T	B	O	O	O	D	A	T	S	Y	■	PUSS IN BOOTS

THE MESSAGE IS: Cinderella had a ball and you will too if you like to read fairytales. Read a fairytale today.

NOTES:_____

_____

_____

_____

_____

_____

_____

A MYSTERY MESSAGE FOR FAIRYTALE EXPERTS

> If you have read many fairytales (both old and modern) you should be able to solve the mystery below. Cross off the name of each fairytale described below in the grid. The remaining letters will spell a message.

1. The princess in this fairytale should never have tried to learn to spin.
2. The girl in this story needed to be very careful about watching the time.
3. The girl in this story took a trip to a strange land in a flying house.
4. This more modern fairytale was written by Collodi.
5. The two children in this fairytale had a sweet tooth, unfortunately for them.
6. Seven was a lucky number for this beautiful black-haired princess.
7. The princess in this fairytale should have been more careful about where she threw her golden ball.
8. The animal in this fairytale pretended to be a noblemen with many acres of land in order to help his master, the youngest son in a family.

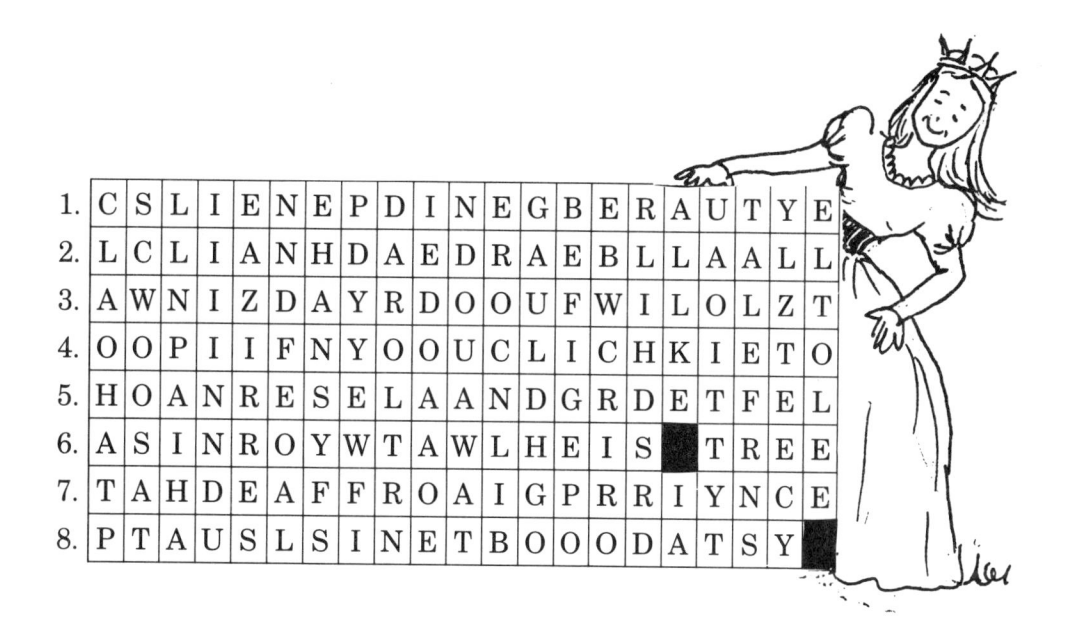

1.| C	S	L	I	E	N	E	P	D	I	N	E	G	B	E	R	A	U	T	Y	E
2.| L	C	L	I	A	N	H	D	A	E	D	R	A	E	B	L	L	A	A	L	L
3.| A	W	N	I	Z	D	A	Y	R	D	O	O	U	F	W	I	L	O	L	Z	T
4.| O	O	P	I	I	F	N	Y	O	O	U	C	L	I	C	H	K	I	E	T	O
5.| H	O	A	N	R	E	S	E	L	A	A	N	D	G	R	D	E	T	F	E	L
6.| A	S	I	N	R	O	Y	W	T	A	W	L	H	E	I	S	■	T	R	E	E
7.| T	A	H	D	E	A	F	F	R	O	A	I	G	P	R	R	I	Y	N	C	E
8.| P	T	A	U	S	L	S	I	N	E	T	B	O	O	O	D	A	T	S	Y	■

AND THE MESSAGE IS:_____

_____

_____

_____

_____

_____

Name_____   Grade_____

TEACHER'S PAGE FOR "FAIRYTALE ACTIVITIES"

GRADE LEVELS: 3–6
SKILLS USED: Creativity, Creative Writing, Knowledge of Fairytales

This activity page should be given to the students a week to two weeks before the projects are due. Require that they pick their project at least a week before it is due. Most of these activities would be done at home and then brought to school. It is a good activity to do on the last day of a fairytale unit. You will be surprised at the creativity some students display in their projects. Videotaping the projects adds interest and incentive for the students.

If you do not wish to make this a homework assignment, you might use the different activities as classroom activities.

For example: It would be fun to construct a fairytale castle as a group. Have students bring various sized boxes and paper towel cores. Furnish many miniature marshmallows and the "cement" frosting (recipe is given. Be sure to bring enough marshmallows for the one or two that each student will sample!). You might want to get some aide or volunteer help and divide the class into groups and let one or two groups work on a castle and other groups work on gingerbread houses. Individual gingerbread houses can also be made by having students use graham crackers to construct the house, cementing each piece with the "cement" frosting and then decorating with different types of candies.

Activity 3 could be a class activity with each student coming to class as a fairytale character and telling the class something about his or her character but not everything, so that the class must guess who the character is. This would also be a good activity for the last day of a fairytale unit.

Activity 5 could be done as a class creative writing assignment.

Activities 6 and 7 would make good classroom activities by having each student write one fairytale news item for the newspaper or newscast.

Activity 9 could also be a class assignment. Have each student find a recipe for the cookbook and then change the recipe by renaming it with a fairytale name (example: scrambled eggs could be Rumpelstiltskin's gold) and also renaming the ingredients (example: sugar could be fairyland snow, etc.). The recipes could be copied so that each child would have all of the recipes, and then each student assemble the recipes into his or her own cookbook and make the cover for the book.

The students will have fun with these activities and I think you will too!

FAIRYTALE ACTIVITIES

CHOOSE ONE OF THE FOLLOWING ACTIVITIES TO DO. BE READY TO SHOW YOUR ACTIVITY OR TO DO IT FOR THE CLASS.

1. Construct a castle out of mini-marshmallows. Make a form out of cardboard boxes and paper towel cores. Put the marshmallows around the castle like the stones found in a real castle. Use a mortar or powdered sugar (recipe below). Ice cream cones or cone-shaped paper cups could be used for the tops of the turrets. You may also devise a castle using your own ideas.
2. Construct a gingerbread house like the one in HANSEL AND GRETEL. Use the mortar made of powdered sugar. The recipe is below.
3. Dress as a fairytale character. Tell your story to the class from your character's point of view.
4. Make a fairytale puppet and demonstrate the puppet to the class.
5. Write a space age fairytale. Illustrate your story and then show it to the class.
6. Pretend you are a newscaster and tell some exciting news from a fairytale. You could pretend to be announcing the news of the giant being robbed and tell what was stolen from him and the suspect's description (JACK AND THE BEANSTALK). You could describe the witch in a fairytale and then tell what she is wanted for or how to avoid her. There are many things that happen in fairytales which could make a news story. Have at least three news stories in your broadcast.
7. Write a fairytale land newspaper, including items from various newspapers written as newspaper articles.
8. Make a diorama of a favorite fairytale.
9. Make a fairytale cookbook.
10. Make several fairytale clothespin characters. Dress them in appropriate costumes and mount them on a cardboard stand.

I chose activity # _____

CEMENT FROSTING:

1 box powdered sugar
3 egg whites, room temperature
1/2 tsp. cream of tartar

Beat 8-10 minutes until stiff peaks.

Name_____

Grade_____

E. Research Activities for Winter

TEACHER'S PAGE AND KEY FOR "HOLIDAY BOOK SCRAMBLE"

GRADE LEVELS: 3–6

This activity with its mixed-up book titles involves both thinking skills and card catalog usage.

The students are first to unscramble the titles and then use the card catalog to find the author of each.

If used in a class, copy enough activities for each class member. On the blackboard or on a bulletin board write or post a mixed-up title—THE CAT IN THE HAT might be a good one since it is easy—ETH TAC NI ETH AHT. Let the students try to figure out that title and then explain that they are to do the same thing in HOLIDAY SCRAMBLE.

Hopefully there will not be too big a crowd at the card catalog since the students will be finishing at different times. If you have a large group, you might have some use the card catalog after each title is unscrambled and others wait until the entire page is complete.

If you wish to do this activity as a media center/library activity or contest, prepare real gift packages or make them from construction paper and mount them on a bulletin board. Put a scrambled book title on each package and then let students unscramble the titles and find the authors. Since this would be a voluntary and not a required activity, awarding a small prize or a bookmark to each student completing the activity would be appropriate.

> KEY: 1. *Ramona the Pest* by Beverly Cleary 2. *Superfudge* by Judy Blume 3. *The Black Stallion* by Walter Farley 4. *Call of the Wild* by Jack London 5. *King of the Wind* by Marguerite Henry 6. *The Hero and the Crown* by Robin McKinley 7. *The Wizard of Oz* by L. Frank Baum 8. *The Great Brain* by John Fitzgerald 9. *The Indian in the Cupboard* by Lynn Reid Banks 10. *The Wind in the Willows* by Kenneth Grahame 11. *Buddies* by Barbara Park 12. *Gentle Ben* by Walt Morey

NOTES:

A HOLIDAY BOOK SCRAMBLE

Gifts are fun to get at Christmas, Hannakuh, or birthdays and books make a great gift. Below are some packages which contain books but their titles are scrambled. See if you can unscramble them!

1. maroan hte espt
2. fuspreugde
3. het labkc lastloni
4. alcl fo eth liwd
5. gnik fo eht niwd
6. hte rohe nad eth cowrn
7. hte dazirw fo zo
8. hte trega arbin
9. eth dinnai ni het pubocrad
10. eth ndwi ni het slowilw
11. dubisde
12. leentg enb

Name_____ Grade_____

E. Research Activities for Winter

TEACHER'S PAGE AND KEY FOR "HOLIDAY RESEARCH A & B"

GRADE LEVELS: A—Grades 3 & 4
        B—Grades 5–8

 These two activities provide different levels of research so that you may choose the activity best suited to your group of children. HOLIDAY RESEARCH A involves using the card catalog and the dictionary. HOLIDAY RESEARCH B involves using a book of quotations, *Famous First Facts,* the card catalog, the encyclopedia, and *The Guinness Book of World Records.*

 Either activity can be used as an individual choice activity in the classroom, media center, or library by making a large green tree out of construction paper and mounting it on a bulletin board. Make different-colored ornaments from construction paper and write one of the questions on each ornament. Students could then answer the questions during their free time during the month of December. A small prize or a bookmark could be awarded to each student completing the activity. Posting names of these ambitious students is an added incentive for others to participate next time.

 If used as a classroom activity it might be well to start students on different numbers in order to avoid congestion at the card catalog or at any particular reference source.

KEY TO HOLIDAY RESEARCH A: 1. Clement Moore (Card Catalog) 2. Candy (Dictionary) 3. Edna Miller (Card Catalog) 4. France (Dictionary) 5. Random House (Card Catalog)

KEY TO HOLIDAY RESEARCH B: 1. Edmund Hamilton (*Bartlett's Familiar Quotations*) 2. Richard S. Pease (*Famous First Facts*) 3. Varies (Card Catalog) 4. Italy (*World Book*—under CHRISTMAS) 5. December 13th—St. Lucia Day (*World Book* under CHRISTMAS) 6. Anonymous (*Bartlett's Familiar Quotations* 7. 221-foot douglas fir—Northgate Shopping Center in Seattle, WA, Dec. 1950 (*1985 Guinness Book of World Records*) 8. 103,152 were at a party given by Boeing in Seattle, WA. on Dec. 15, 1979 (*Guinness Book of World Records*) 9. THE CHRISTMAS PINATA or THE 12 DAYS OF CHRISTMAS (Card Catalog) 10. Card Catalog.

NOTES:_____
_____

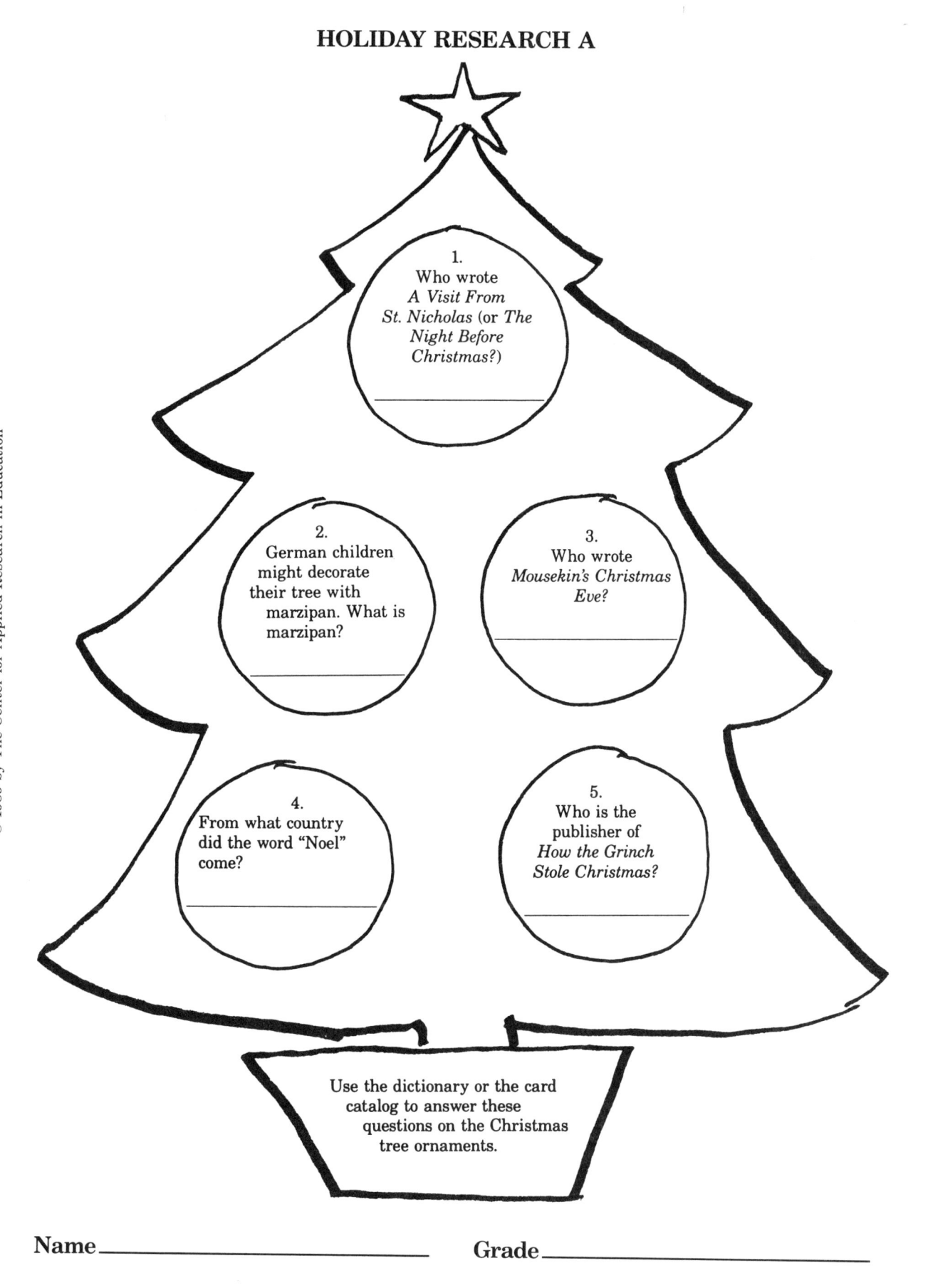

HOLIDAY RESEARCH A

1. Who wrote *A Visit From St. Nicholas* (or *The Night Before Christmas?*)
   _____

2. German children might decorate their tree with marzipan. What is marzipan?
   _____

3. Who wrote *Mousekin's Christmas Eve?*
   _____

4. From what country did the word "Noel" come?
   _____

5. Who is the publisher of *How the Grinch Stole Christmas?*
   _____

Use the dictionary or the card catalog to answer these questions on the Christmas tree ornaments.

Name _____ Grade _____

© 1989 by The Center for Applied Research in Education

HOLIDAY RESEARCH B

Answer these questions on the tree by using reference sources. Color each ornament as you answer the question nearest it.

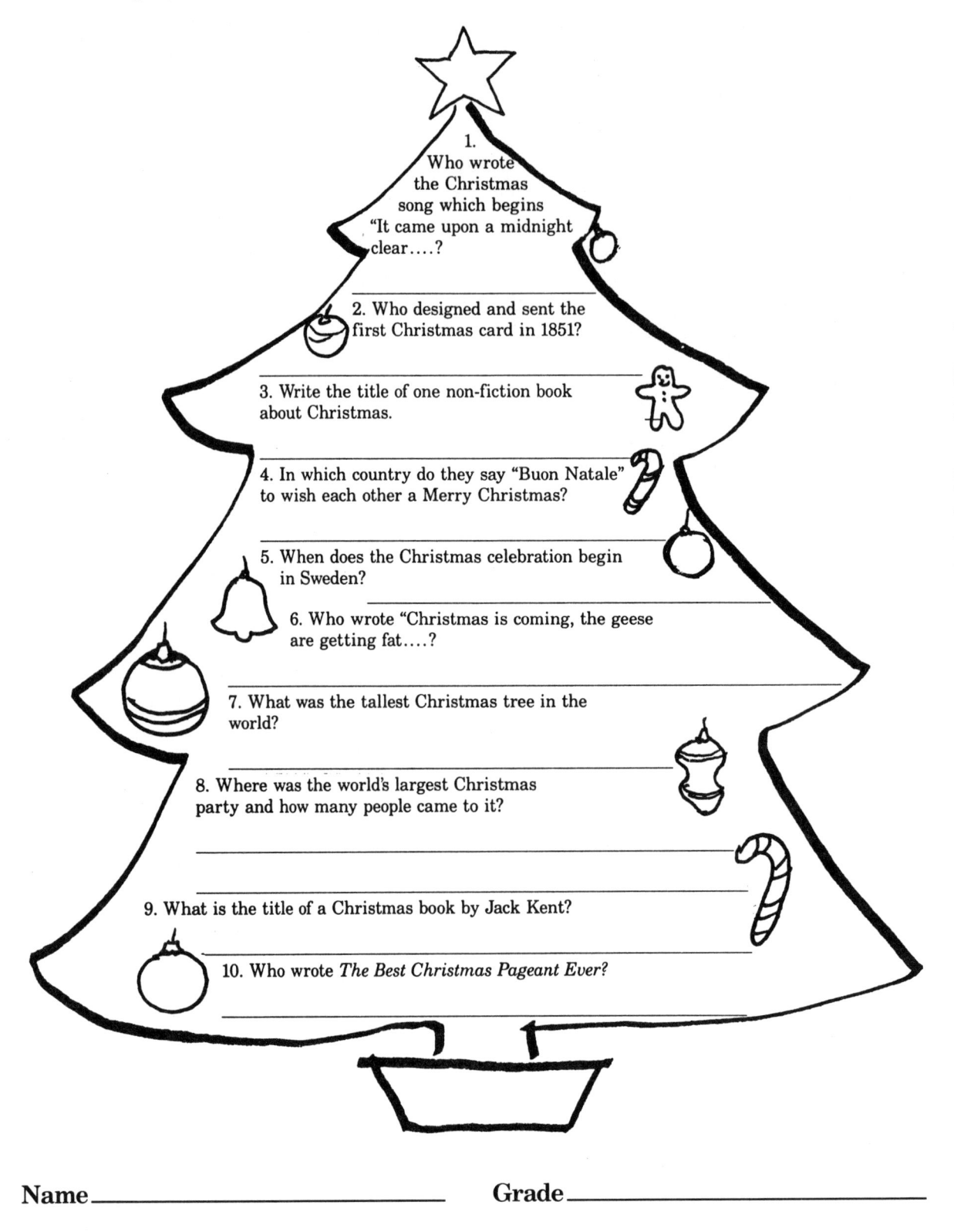

1. Who wrote the Christmas song which begins "It came upon a midnight clear...?

2. Who designed and sent the first Christmas card in 1851?

3. Write the title of one non-fiction book about Christmas.

4. In which country do they say "Buon Natale" to wish each other a Merry Christmas?

5. When does the Christmas celebration begin in Sweden?

6. Who wrote "Christmas is coming, the geese are getting fat....?

7. What was the tallest Christmas tree in the world?

8. Where was the world's largest Christmas party and how many people came to it?

9. What is the title of a Christmas book by Jack Kent?

10. Who wrote *The Best Christmas Pageant Ever?*

Name_____ Grade_____

© 1989 by The Center for Applied Research in Education

E. Research Activities for Winter

TEACHER'S PAGE AND KEY FOR "WHO SAID IT?"

GRADE LEVELS: 5–8

This activity could be used in a library skills class for extra practice with the book of quotations, or it could be used in the Media Center or classroom as a contest or extra-credit activity.

As a class activity in the Media Center, unless you have quite a few books of quotations, you may wish to have half of the class work on the activity while the other half finds and checks out books. In the next class session, the tasks could be reversed with the group which had worked with the activity finding and checking out books while the other group does the research.

As a Media Center or classroom contest or extra credit activity, enlarge the Santa. Color him with felt-tip pens. Cut large ornaments from bright-colored construction paper. Print a quotation on each or type the quotation and mount one on each ornament. Make large construction paper letters or use plastic point-back letters or form the words, "Who Said It?"

Allow extra credit to each student completing the activity or award a small prize or bookmark to each student ambitious enough to complete the activity.

> KEY: (All Quotations can be located in *Bartlett's Familiar Quotations* under the heading "Christmas.")
> 1. Robert Southwell
> 2. Charles Dickens
> 3. Irving Berlin
> 4. Thomas Tusser
> 5. Clement Moore
> 6. Anonymous

NOTES:

WHO SAID IT?

Use a book of quotations to help you find out who said these things about Christmas.

1. "And straight I called unto mind that it was Christmas Day."
   _____

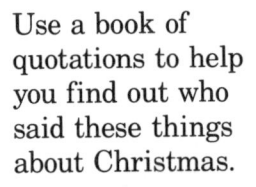

2. "I will honor Christmas in my heart, and try to keep it all the year."
   _____

3. "I'm dreaming of a white Christmas, Just like the ones I used to know,"
   _____

4. "At Christmas play and make good cheer, For Christmas comes but once a year."
   _____

5. "T'was the night before Christmas, And all through the house, Not a creature was stirring, Not even a mouse."
   _____

6. "Christmas is coming, The goose is getting fat, Please to put a penny in the old man's hat."
   _____

Name _____

Grade _____

© 1989 by The Center for Applied Research in Education

E. Research Activities for Winter

TEACHER'S PAGE FOR "DECEMBER DICTIONARY FUN"

GRADE LEVELS: 3 and 4 (possibly 2nd)

This activity is done in the same way that HALLOWEEN FUN WITH THE DICTIONARY and THANKSGIVING ART AND RESEARCH in Unit I were done.

Read the directions with the class and then let the children work independently. Some students may need to be reminded that there is an additional direction, #5 underneath the four more obvious squares. Provide crayons or felt-tip pens and encourage the students to do their best. Remind them that they will be showing their illustrations to the rest of the class. Children who finish early might be asked to use all five of the words in a sentence or paragraph. Be sure to allow them to read these sentences and paragraphs after the illustrations are shown.

Additional activity: Give the students a blank piece of paper and a dictionary. Have them find a new word which they think the class will not already know. Some children may be directed even more specifically to find a new word which they can use in connection with the holiday season. Tell them to write the word in a sentence at the bottom of their blank page. They are to underline the word which is new to them. Then they should illustrate the sentence they wrote. When all or most of the students are finished, let each one read their sentence, show their illustration, and challenge the class to guess the meaning of the underlined word.

> KEY: Box 1: A very happy Santa should be drawn Box 2: A tiny elf should be in this box Box 3: A girl carrying a very large gift Box 4: A boy carrying a very tiny gift.

DECEMBER DICTIONARY FUN

Use the dictionary to look up the underlined words in each box below. Then draw in the box what the directions tell you to do. Put the guide words from the page where you found the underlined words in the blanks in each box.

1. _____ _____

Make a *jovial* Santa in this box.

2. _____ _____

Make a *wisp* of an elf in this box.

3. _____ _____

Make a girl carrying a *titanic* gift in this box.

4. _____ _____

Make a boy carrying a *minuscule* gift in this box.

5. Make a December *landscape* on the back of this page.

Name _____ **Grade** _____

© 1989 by The Center for Applied Research in Education

E. Research Activities for Winter

TEACHER'S PAGE FOR "HAPPY NEW YEAR"

GRADE LEVELS: Any grade familiar with almanacs and encyclopedias
SKILLS USED: Research in almanac

All of the answers in "Happy New Year" may be found in the *World Almanac* so the activity could be used for additional practice in using the almanac. The activity could also be used for research skills practice by letting the students decide for themselves which reference source is best. Some of the answers can also be found in encyclopedias.

After the activity is completed, you may wish to let the children read their resolutions from the activity. Another activity which would be fun would be to let each student make up a resolution for some fictional character. Then let each student read their resolution and see if the class can guess the name of the character making the resolution.

If you need any examples to get the class started, you might use:

"I will never tell another lie. My nose is just the right size already." (Pinocchio)

"I will stop pulling Susan's curls even if I do like the way they go 'boink.'" (Ramona in *Ramona, the Pest* by Cleary)

"I resolve that I will leave Peter's pets alone, especially if he gets another turtle." (Fudge in *Tales of a Fourth Grade Nothing* by Blume)

"I resolve to have no water in my castle at all because a little bit might kill me." (The Wicked Witch of the West from *The Wizard of Oz* by Baum.)

KEY FOR "HAPPY NEW YEAR"
1. Sally Field 2. James Tobin 3. Ronald Reagan 4. Alan B. Shepard, Jr. 5. Dorothy Hamill 6. Harper Lee 7. Susan Powell (Elks City, Oklahoma) 8. Jonas Salk 9. Michael Jackson for "Beat It" 10. Samuel Morse

HAPPY NEW YEAR!

Many people make New Year Resolutions—promises to do something or to quit something in the coming year. Most people do not keep their resolutions, but if the resolutions below had been made by some famous people, they would have been kept! SEE IF YOU CAN DISCOVER THE NAMES OF THE FAMOUS PEOPLE BY USING REFERENCE SOURCES.

1. I resolve to be voted the Academy Award for Best Actress in 1984. _____
2. I resolve to win the Nobel Prize for Economics in 1981._____
3. I resolve to be elected President of the United States in 1980._____
4. I resolve to be the first American in Space in 1961._____
5. I resolve to win the Olympic gold medal for women's singles in figure skating in 1976._____
6. I resolve to win the Pulitzer Prize for fiction in 1961 with my book *To Kill a Mockingbird*._____
7. I resolve to be voted Miss America in 1981._____
8. I resolve to discover the vaccine which will help cure Polio in 1953. _____
9. I resolve to win the Grammy award for the best record in 1983. _____ for the record_____
10. I resolve to invent the magnetic telegraph in 1837._____

NOW SUPPOSE YOU COULD DO OR BE ANYONE YOU WANTED IN THE NEXT YEAR. WHAT WOULD YOUR NEW YEAR'S RESOLUTION BE?

_____

_____

_____

_____

_____

_____

_____

_____

Name_____ **Grade**_____

© 1989 by The Center for Applied Research in Education

E. Research Activities for Winter

TEACHER'S PAGE FOR "THE CHINESE ZODIAC"

GRADE LEVELS: 3–6
SKILLS: RESEARCH AND CREATIVE WRITING

Children usually think it is fun to hear about the Chinese Zodiac with its 12-year animal cycle.

Tell the students about the 12-year animal cycle. Those who are familiar with our zodiac with its 12-month cycle might compare them. You might introduce the activity by reading a book such as *The Rat, the Ox, and the Zodiac* by Dorothy Van Woerkom. After the discussion about the zodiac and the dates of the Chinese New Year, have the children pick out their animal sign from the chart on the activity page. Since most of them will be near the same age, most will have the same animal sign. If this will cause a shortage of reference material you could, instead, assign an animal for each child to research instead of the animal of his own year of birth. Explain to the students that some Chinese believe that the animal sign of the year of birth helps determine the person's character and life. Explain that each animal has good and bad qualities and tell the students to point out both good and bad qualities of the animal they research.

An extra activity could be for each child to take a poll of their own family to find the animal sign for each. When the signs are brought back to school, the class could compile them into a chart showing how many family members have each of the 12 signs. An additional activity could be to have the children research Chinese New Year activities which are interesting and which last for several days.

Reference Sources: Encyclopedias *Books: The Rat, the Ox, and the Zodiac* adapted by Dorothy Van Woerkom, Crown ©1976. *The Chinese New Year* by Cheng Hou-Tien, Holt Owlet ©1976.

THE CHINESE ZODIAC

The Chinese New Year falls somewhere between January 21st and February 20th. Their zodiac, unlike our 12-month one, is a 12-year cycle. Each year is represented by an animal. Some believe that the year in which you are born helps determine your character and your life. An animal represents each year of the 12-year cycle, and its good and bad qualities are supposed to be a part of the character of people born within that year. Below are the 12 animals of the Chinese Zodiac and the years of each. Find out which animal represents the year in which you were born. Draw a picture of that animal and then look up your animal in an encyclopedia or reference book. Write a short report about it.

THE RAT: 1960, 1972, 1984, 1996
THE TIGER: 1974, 1986, 1998
THE DRAGON: 1964, 1976, 1988, 2000
THE HORSE: 1966, 1978, 1990, 2002
THE MONKEY: 1968, 1980, 1992, 2004
THE DOG: 1970, 1982, 1994, 2006

THE OX: 1961, 1973, 1985, 1997
THE RABBIT: 1963, 1975, 1987, 1999
THE SNAKE: 1965, 1977, 1989, 2001
THE SHEEP: 1967, 1979, 1991, 2003
THE COCK: 1969, 1981, 1993, 2005
THE BOAR: 1971, 1983, 1995, 2007

MY ANIMAL IS THE: _____

_____
_____
_____
_____

Name_____   Grade_____

© 1989 by The Center for Applied Research in Education

E. Research Activities for Winter

TEACHER'S PAGE FOR
"VALENTINES FOR FAMOUS PEOPLE"

GRADE LEVELS: 4–6
SKILLS: Research skills in almanac, card catalog, and encyclopedia

After reading the directions with the children and discussing them, let the children decide what reference books they are going to need to find who the valentines will be given to. Explain that for number 11, each student is to find some famous people and write what they did.

It would be fun to give each student a piece of red construction paper and let them cut out a heart and then with felt-tip pen write something that a famous person has done. The famous person's name should be put on the back. Mount these hearts and then during the next class period let the class see how many of the famous people they can discover.

They could also make a valentine for their favorite author and these too could be mounted on the bulletin board. Then in a subsequent class period, students could try to find a book title for each author who has a valentine on the bulletin board.

> KEY: 1. John Christopher
> 2. Maurice Sendak
> 3. Morrow
> 4. Tom Watson
> 5. Chris Evert
> 6. Wade Boggs
> 7. Steve Sax
> 8. Trina Schart Hyman
> 9. Pierre Curie and Marie Curie
> 10. Robin McKinley

NOTES:_____
_____
_____
_____
_____

VALENTINES FOR FAMOUS PEOPLE

Sometimes famous people are so busy they don't have time for holidays like Valentines day. See if you can discover the names of the famous people who deserved a valentine for the things they did.

1. A valentine to the author of *The White Mountains*. _____

2. A valentine to the illustrator of *Where the Wild Things Are*. _____

3. A valentine to the publisher of *Ramona, the Pest*. _____

4. A valentine to the winner of the men's United States Open Golf Tournament in 1982. _____

5. A valentine to the winner of the women's United States Open Tennis Singles Championship in 1978. _____

6. A valentine to the batting champion in baseball's American League in 1985. _____

7. The Rookie of the Year winner in baseball's National League in 1982. _____

8. The winner of the Caldecott Medal in 1985. _____

9. The discoverers of radium. _____ and _____

10. A valentine to the winner of the Newbery Medal in 1985. _____

11. A valentine to _____

Name_____ Grade_____

E. Research Activities for Winter

TEACHER'S PAGE FOR "GREEN IS FOR THE IRISH"

March and St. Patrick's Day presents a good time for additional practice in locating books and in using the card catalog.

Copy the shamrocks on green construction paper and for added use laminate or dry-mount on tagboard. At the end of a 3rd or 4th grade story or skills class, give each child a shamrock and have them locate the book whose call number and title are on the shamrock. For those who need extra practice in using the card catalog, give each child a shamrock with a title on it and tell them that the number of each book has a last name of Green or has "green" in their name. Tell them to find the title in the card catalog, write a good call slip for it, and then find the book.

In case you need more shamrocks with call numbers for books with green in the title here are some other possibilities:

Green Light for Sandy by Carol Morse, *The Green Man* by Haley, *Green Invasion* by Abels, *Green Grass and White Milk* by Aliki, *Green Frontier* by Kormer, *Green Hero: Early Adventures of Finn McCool* by Evslin, *Green Is for Galanx* by Stone, *Green Thirteen* by Ogan, *Green Says Go* by Emberley, *Greenhorn on the Frontier* by Finlayson, *Green of Me* by Gauch, and *Children of Green Knowe* by Lucy Boston, *Greensleeves* by Eloise McGraw.

Other titles which could be put on shamrocks for additional card catalog practice are:

Ask Anybody, Dotty's Suitcase, The Ears of Louis, A Girl Called Al, I and Sproggy, Isabelle Shows Her Stuff, The Unmaking of Rabbit, and *Your Old Pal, Al—* all by Constance Greene.

Where Is Duckling Three? and *Woody the Little Wood Duck* both by Ivah Green, *Rachel's Recital* by Melinda Green, *Nicky's Lopsided, Lumpy, but Delicious Orange* by Phyllis Green, *Kor and the Wolf Dogs* by Robert James Green; *Hi, Clouds!* and *Hinny Winny Bunco* both Carol Greene; *The Mariah Delaney Lending Library Disaster; Matt Pitt and the Tunnel Tenants; The Secret Museum;* and *Valentine Rosy* all by Sheila Greenwald.

Authors of the titles on the shamrocks are: Locating Books: *Green Eggs and Ham* by Dr. Seuss, *Greedy Greeny* by Jack Gantos, *The Green Book* by Jill Paton Walsh, *Green Ginger Jar* by Clara Judson, *The Green Grass Grows all Around* by Hilde Hoffman, *Green Grass of Wyoming* by Mary O'Hara, *The Green Machine* by Polly Cameron, *The Green Man from Space,* by Lewis Zarem, and *The Green Poodles* by Charlotte Baker.

Card Catalog: *Animal Doctors: What Do They Do?* by Carla Greene, *Philip Hall Likes Me. I Reckon Maybe* by Bette Greene, *The Iceberg and Its Shadow* by Jan Greenberg, *Will the Real Gertrude Hollings Please Stand Up* by Sheila Greenwald,

(Continued on next page)

Beat the Turtle Drum and *Double-Dare O'Toole* by Constance Green, *Gloomy Louie* by Phyllis Green, *Isabelle, the Itch* by Constance Greene, and *Rotunda Ate a Cookie* by Vivian Greene.

NOTES:

GREEN IS FOR THE IRISH—LOCATING BOOKS

By using their call numbers have children try to locate these books which have the word "green" in their title.

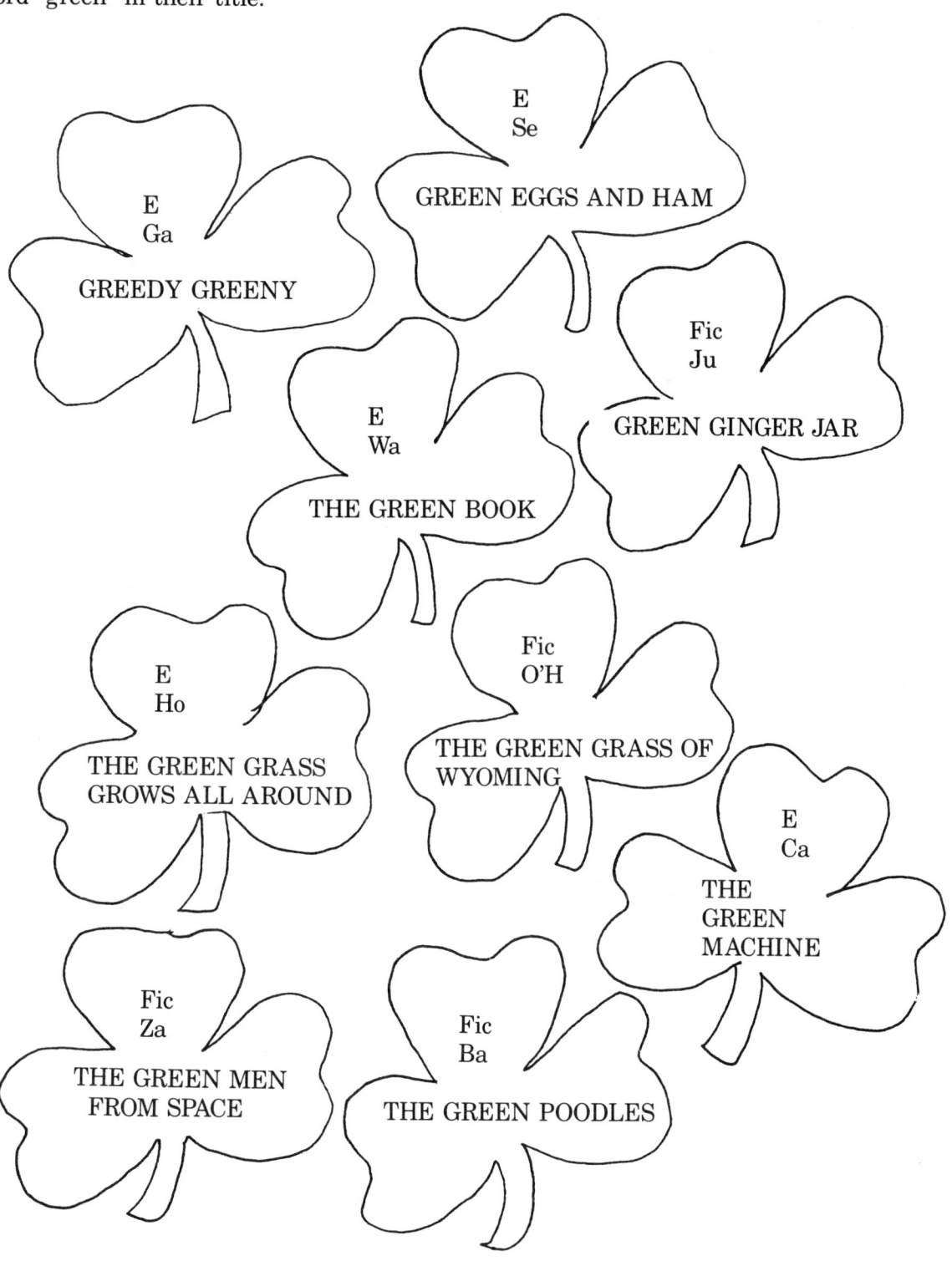

E
Se

GREEN EGGS AND HAM

E
Ga

GREEDY GREENY

Fic
Ju

GREEN GINGER JAR

E
Wa

THE GREEN BOOK

E
Ho

THE GREEN GRASS GROWS ALL AROUND

Fic
O'H

THE GREEN GRASS OF WYOMING

E
Ca

THE GREEN MACHINE

Fic
Za

THE GREEN MEN FROM SPACE

Fic
Ba

THE GREEN POODLES

Name_____   Grade_____

GREEN IS FOR THE IRISH—CARD CATALOG PRACTICE

All of the titles below are for books written by authors whose last name is Green or who have Green in their last name. See if the children can find them in the card catalog, write a good call slip for them, and then find the book. If these titles are not in your card catalog, perhaps your teacher has a copy of *Books in Print* or *Children's Books in Print* which you can use.

- ANIMAL DOCTORS, WHAT DO THEY DO?
- PHILIP HALL LIKES ME, I RECKON MAYBE
- THE ICEBERG AND ITS SHADOW
- WILL THE REAL GERTRUDE HOLLINGS PLEASE STAND UP?
- BEAT THE TURTLE DRUM
- DOUBLE-DARE O'TOOLE
- GLOOMY LOUIE
- ISABELLE, THE ITCH
- ROTUNDA ATE A COOKIE

Name_____ Grade_____

© 1989 by The Center for Applied Research in Education

GREEN IS FOR THE IRISH—BLANK SHAMROCK PATTERNS

Use these blank shamrock patterns to make your own call slips which fit your particular collection.

Name _____ Grade _____

TEACHER'S PAGE FOR
"A ST. PATRICK'S DAY JOURNEY"

"A St. Patrick's Day Journey" is an activity involving knowledge of the Dewey Decimal System and the shelving of these numbered books. Students are to read the story and find the answers for the blanks by finding the shelf where the books have the same number as that found beneath the blank. They should then be able to tell what answer goes in the blank.

In a class situation, in order to avoid congestion, students could each begin on a different sentence, realizing that they are to fill in all of the blanks and not just the one on which they begin.

Talented or able students could write a story like this on their own. You could assign them a number such as 796.33 for football or 636.1 for horses and see if they can write a story using at least five blanks with an answer to be found by using a Dewey Decimal number which they are to put beneath the blank.

Give the class a certain number of minutes to fill in the blanks and then let the class read the story aloud before the class is over. If any students have written good Dewey Decimal stories of their own, it would be nice to type them, make copies, and let the class figure them out too.

KEY:	holiday	airplane	Oregon	stars
	weather	cars	magic	basketball
	dog	bird	cat	holiday

NOTES:_____

_____

_____

_____

_____

_____

_____

_____

A ST. PATRICK'S DAY JOURNEY

Name_____ **Grade**_____

    Jim was excited. St. Patrick's Day was only three days away and it was his favorite (394) _____. It was to be especially nice this year for he was going to get to take a (629.13) _____ and go to see his grandparents in (979.5) _____.

    Grandmother had said that they would get to go to the Museum of Science and Industry and see a special show on (523.4) _____.

    Jim hoped that the (551.5) _____ would be good because there was a big parade on Saturday and Jim would get to ride in one of the (629.2) _____ in the parade.

    After the parade there was going to be a (793.5) _____ show and the next day he would get to see a (796.32) _____ game.

    Besides all this fun Jim just liked to visit his grandparents. He loved them and their (636.7) _____ too. He even liked their (598.2) _____. He especially like their (636.8) _____ named Tuffy who liked to sleep on the foot of his bed.

    Yes, this St. Patrick's Day would be special and Jim could hardly wait for it to come.

NOW WRITE A SENTENCE OR TWO ABOUT YOUR FAVORITE (394) _____.

_____
_____

TELL WHY YOU LIKE IT. _____
_____
_____
_____
_____
_____
_____
_____

TEACHER'S DIRECTIONS FOR
HELP THE LEPRECHAUN FIND THE POT OF GOLD

This activity involves work in the almanac or the encyclopedia. Most answers can be found in either of the reference sources but don't tell the students where to look. Let each child determine for his or herself which is the proper resource. Since most libraries have an adequate number of almanacs, there should not be too much congestion around the reference shelves.

In another class, another activity which would be fun to do would be to give each student a path drawn on paper such as the ones in *Help the Leprechaun Find the Pot of Gold* or in *Can You Beat the Witch to the Pumpkin Patch?* in Unit I. Have each student draw a person or animal at the top of the page and something the animal or person would like at the bottom. Then let them figure out questions for the spaces in the path. Giving each student an almanac and having them find their questions in it would make a quieter work time, but allowing them to use any reference source makes them think a little more. If they need suggestions you might suggest that they draw a bear at the top of the page and a pot of honey at the bottom, or a prince at the top of the page and a castle and a beautiful princess at the bottom. Let the class make some suggestions before the students begin and there will be many ideas.

> KEY: 1. Green, white, and red   2. Dublin   3. Tuesday
> 4. 3,575,000   5. 27, 137   6. 47 (*1986 Almanac*)
> 7. 60 inches (encyclopedia)   8. Samuel Beckett
> 9. Early 400s to 461 (*World Book* under Ireland—also in the *Almanac*   10. Prime Minister

NOTES:

HELP THE LEPRECHAUN FIND THE POT OF GOLD!

Answer each question until you and the leprechaun have reached the pot of gold!

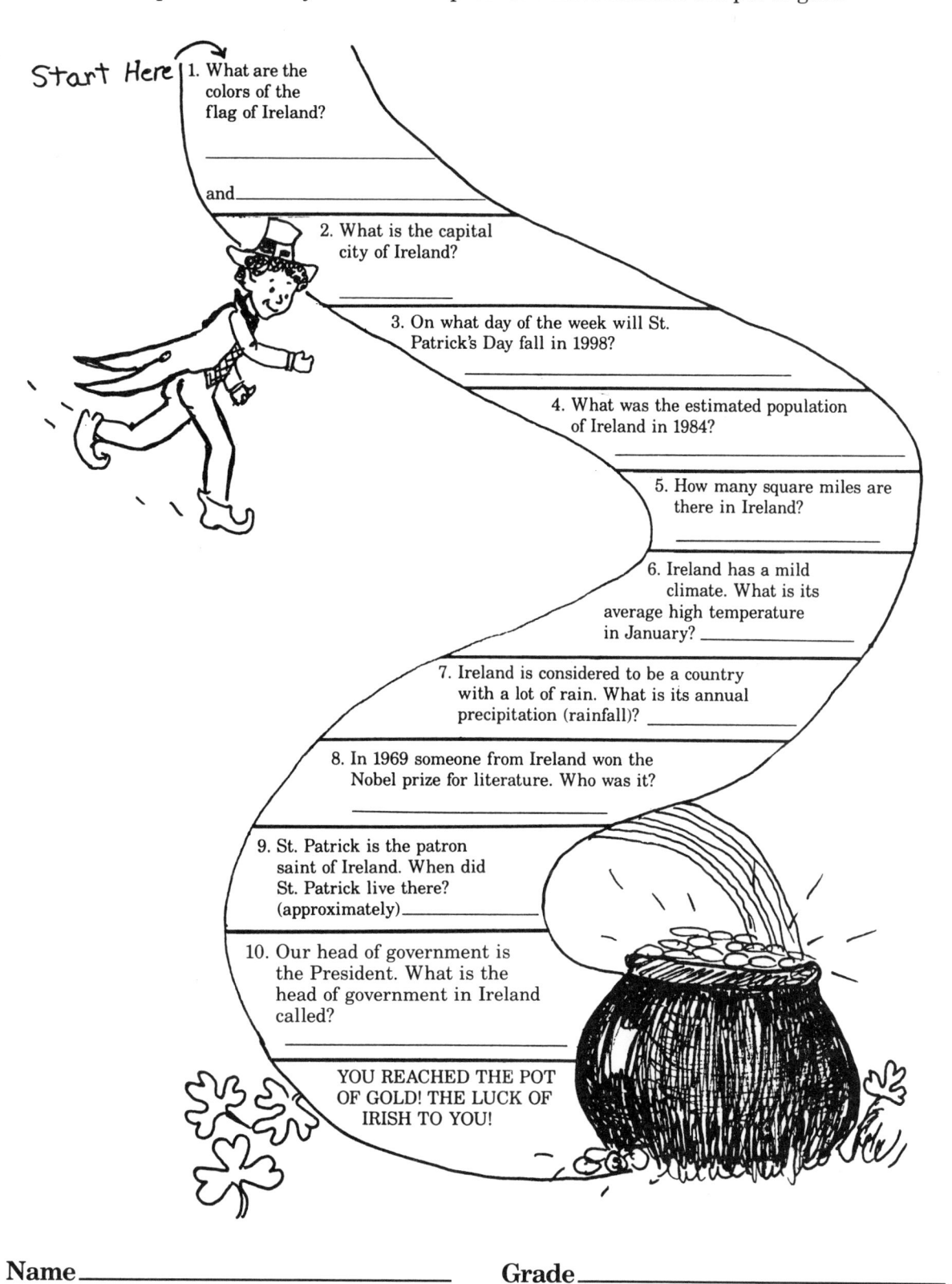

Start Here

1. What are the colors of the flag of Ireland?
   _____
   and _____

2. What is the capital city of Ireland?
   _____

3. On what day of the week will St. Patrick's Day fall in 1998?
   _____

4. What was the estimated population of Ireland in 1984?
   _____

5. How many square miles are there in Ireland?
   _____

6. Ireland has a mild climate. What is its average high temperature in January? _____

7. Ireland is considered to be a country with a lot of rain. What is its annual precipitation (rainfall)? _____

8. In 1969 someone from Ireland won the Nobel prize for literature. Who was it?
   _____

9. St. Patrick is the patron saint of Ireland. When did St. Patrick live there? (approximately) _____

10. Our head of government is the President. What is the head of government in Ireland called?
    _____

YOU REACHED THE POT OF GOLD! THE LUCK OF IRISH TO YOU!

Name _____   Grade _____

© 1989 by The Center for Applied Research in Education

Spring Activities

UNIT III

Activity — *Skills Used*

A. SPRING READING BINGOS — Reading Appreciation
Directions for Spring Reading Bingos

I LOVE BOOKS READING BINGO
Teacher Directions
Student Bingo Card
Bulletin Board Squares
Bookmarks and Notes from Home
Certificate

LET'S TRAVEL READING BINGO
Teacher Directions
Student Bingo Card
Bulletin Board Squares
Bookmarks and Notes from Home
Certificate

B. ANIMAL READING PROGRAM FOR THE PRIMARY GRADES — Reading Promotion
Teacher Directions
Student Record Sheet
Animal Record Patterns
Student Notes for Home

Activity   *Skills Used*

C. SPRING STUDENT DETECTIVE
    ACTIVITIES

THE STUDENT DETECTIVE
AND THE CASE OF THE APRIL
FOOL JOKER
Teacher Directions and Key
Student Activity Page
Certificates

Almanac, *Famous First Facts*,
Encyclopedia, *Guinness Book of
World Records*

THE STUDENT DETECTIVE
AND THE CASE OF THE
MYSTERY INVITATION
Teacher Directions and Key
Student Activity Page
Certificates

Almanac, Dictionary, Encyclopedia

D. SPRING CROSSWORD COUNT
    PUZZLES
Directions and Record of Scores for
    Spring Crossword Count Puzzles

WELCOME SPRING CROSSWORD
COUNT
Student Activity Page
Certificates

Dictionary and Thinking Skills

A BUSY TIME FOR BEES
CROSSWORD COUNT
Student Activity Page
Certificates

Dictionary and Thinking Skills

E. RESEARCH ACTIVITIES FOR
    SPRING

SPRINGTIME IS BIRD TIME
Teacher Directions and Key
Student Activity Page

Almanac, Card Catalog

HELP THE BUNNY FIND HIS
BASKET
Teacher Directions and Key
Student Activity Page

Almanac, Dictionary

DICTIONARY FUN FOR
MOTHER'S DAY
Teacher Directions and Key
Student Activity Page

Dictionary

Spring Activities

Activity	*Skills Used*
IT HAPPENED IN THE SPRINGTIME Teacher Directions and Key Student Activity Page	Almanac
A SUMMER VACATION IN CANADA Teacher Directions and Key Student Activity Page	Encyclopedia, Almanac, *Guinness Book of World Records*
HIP, HIP, HOORAY FOR FATHER'S DAY Teacher Directions and Key Student Activity Page	Dewey Decimal System, Card Catalog
THROUGH THE SUMMERTIME Teacher Directions and Key Student Activity Page	Almanac, Encyclopedia, Thesaurus, or Dictionary

A. Spring Reading Bingos

DIRECTIONS FOR SPRING READING BINGOS

The Spring Reading Bingos, "I Love Books" and "Let's Travel," could be used at any time of the year, but "I Love Books" is appropriate for use in April because National Library Week occurs then. (It is also useful in November during National Children's Book Week.) "Let's Travel" is appropriate for May since summer vacation time is near.

The general directions on how to use the bingos are printed with the Autumn bingos. Refer to these directions if you have not used the bingos before.

DIRECTIONS FOR "I LOVE BOOKS READING BINGO"

The "I LOVE BOOKS READING BINGO" encourages students to read in different areas such as science fiction, humor, adventure, poetry, etc. It might be good to introduce this bingo in correlation with activities for National Library Week, but it could be used at any time of the year.

If children need some suggestions for the various categories you might suggest the following: Science Fiction: Books by Madeleine L'Engle or John Christopher for very good readers; books by Andre Norton (several different reading levels), and for children needing easier reading levels the science fiction books of Alfred Slote. For humor: Books by Beverly Cleary, some by Judy Blume, Barbara Parks, Clifford Hicks, and Robert Peck. Adventure Books, Classics such as *Kidnapped* or *The Adventures of Tom Sawyer* for good readers, some of the non-sport books of Matt Christopher for students needing easier reading, and Eloise McGraw and Walt Morey for good readers. Historical Fiction: Elizabeth Speare, Lincoln Collier, and Janet Lunn for good readers. Easier books in this genre are those written by such authors as Laura Ingalls Wilder or Doris Gates. Many Newbery medal winning books are historical fiction books. Poetry: Children love the poetry books of Shel Silverstein and Jack Prelutsky, but there are many more in the poetry section of the library. Lead them to 808.1 and let them pick out their own. Mystery: Books by Florence Heide, Zilpha Snyder, or Peggy Parrish offer a wide range of ability levels in the mystery genre. Arts and Crafts: Direct the children to the 745 section in your library and let them pick out their own arts and crafts book. It might be fun to have them bring something which they have made following directions in the book they read instead of a note from home to show they have read the book. Animal Books:

Walt Morey, Doris Gates, Jim Kjelgaard, and Marguerite Henry are a few of the many authors who have written animal books for different levels of ability. Biography: The 921 section can yield biographies for all levels of ability. Let them choose their own. Sports Books: Recommend authors such as Matt Christopher (easy reading), Alfred Slote (middle readers) or Tunis (difficult).

The above suggestions are but a few suggestions which might be made in the various levels. Most children will be able to find their own books for each.

Once the bingo has begun, the bingo card could be stamped with a heart, a flower, or any stamp which you have which might symbolize a love of books.

An appropriate prize for bingo winners could be a movie in the library. The movie could be any which was made from a book, such as *Lassie Come Home, Alice-in-Wonderland, Escape to Witch Mountain, Johnny Tremain*, etc.

The number of each bingo square to enlarge or duplicate for your bulletin board is:

Science Fiction: 3	Humor: 3	Adventure: 2
Historical Fiction: 3	Poetry: 2	Mystery: 3
Arts and Crafts: 2	Animals: 2	Biography: 3
Sports: 2		

NOTES FOR I LOVE BOOKS BINGO: _____

_____

_____

_____

_____

_____

_____

_____

_____

I LOVE BOOKS

READING BINGO

SCIENCE FICTION	HUMOR	ADVENTURE	HISTORICAL FICTION	POETRY
MYSTERY	ARTS AND CRAFTS	ANIMALS	BIOGRAPHY	SPORTS
SPORTS	ADVENTURE	HISTORICAL FICTION	MYSTERY	BIOGRAPHY
ARTS AND CRAFTS	ANIMALS	HUMOR	POETRY	SCIENCE FICTION
HUMOR	HISTORICAL FICTION	BIOGRAPHY	SCIENCE FICTION	MYSTERY

Record the titles of the books you have read in the appropriate square or on the back of this page.

Name_____ **Grade**_____

© 1989 by The Center for Applied Research in Education

SCIENCE FICTION

MYSTERY

SPORTS

HUMOR

ANIMALS

POETRY

"BLOW-SNOW?"

"MOON-JUNE?"

WHERE THE SIDEWALK ENDS

© 1989 by The Center for Applied Research in Education

HISTORICAL FICTION

ARTS AND CRAFTS

BIOGRAPHY

ADVENTURE

© 1989 by The Center for Applied Research in Education

EXPLORE THE FUTURE

READ A SCIENCE FICTION BOOK!

BE A SPORT!

READ A BOOK!

ENJOY AN ADVENTURE

READ A BOOK!

ENJOY A LAUGH!

JOKES

NOTE FROM HOME

_____
(Child's Name)

has read the book:

_____

FOR THE I LOVE BOOKS
      READING BINGO

....
(SIGNATURE OF PARENT OR ANOTHER
 RESPONSIBLE ADULT)

BOOKS

NOTE FROM HOME

_____
(Child's Name)

has read the book:

_____

FOR THE I LOVE BOOKS
      READING BINGO

....
(SIGNATURE OF PARENT OR ANOTHER
 RESPONSIBLE ADULT)

BOOKS

© 1989 by The Center for Applied Research in Education

THIS CERTIFIES THAT

_____

HAS COMPLETED A BINGO IN THE

I Love Books Reading Bingo

_____

Signature of teacher or librarian

© 1989 by The Center for Applied Research in Education

A. Spring Reading Bingos

TEACHER'S PAGE FOR
LET'S TRAVEL READING BINGO

This bingo is suitable for the month of May when students are thinking about summer and vacation time. When the bingo begins, remind students or explain to them that travel in books can also be in time by reading books about the past or the future.

Encourage students to use the card catalog to find their books for this bingo. A few books in each category could be pulled and displayed, but it is good for the students to use the card catalog, and most can be easily found by using subject cards. Books for specific states can be found by looking up the state. There will then be subject cards for that state in both fiction and non-fiction. Other countries will also be found by looking up the specific country desired. Books for the past may be found under historical fiction headings, or look up a specific period such as the Revolutionary War or Colonial Times. Books about the future may be found with a subject title "Future" and fiction titles can be found under Science Fiction.

An extra activity which might be fun for the LET'S TRAVEL READING BINGO might be to give each classroom a cut-out of a locomotive with their class name on it. Have them post it in the hall or library. Each time a child reads a book and marks a bingo square, he or she also receives a car for the class train. The child's name and the title of the book read is then written on the car and the student can add it to the class train. It is usually fun for the students to see whose train is the longest. (This is not necessary in using the bingo, of course, but is an added activity you might like to try.)

When students begin bringing their notes from home their bingo cards could be marked by a sticker or stamp of any type of vehicle—car, train, spaceship, airplane, etc.

At the end of the bingo an appropriate prize might be to issue tickets to all students who bingo for a field trip to an interesting place. Of course, many districts do not have the funds for this or would not approve of it, in which case issue the winners a ticket to come to the library and see a film of some far-off place or a film of space travel or another appropriate film.

The number of squares which you will need to enlarge or duplicate for your bulletin board are:

The Past—Fiction: 3　　　　　　　　The Future—Fiction: 3
Your State—Non-Fiction: 2　　　　　Another Country—Fiction: 3
Space Travel—Non-Fiction: 4　　　　A State in the U. S.—Non-Fiction: 2
The Past—Non-Fiction: 2　　　　　　Another Country—Non-Fiction: 2
A State in the United States—Fiction: 2　　Space Travel—Fiction: 2

NOTES FOR LET'S TRAVEL READING BINGO:

_____

_____

LET'S TRAVEL
READING BINGO

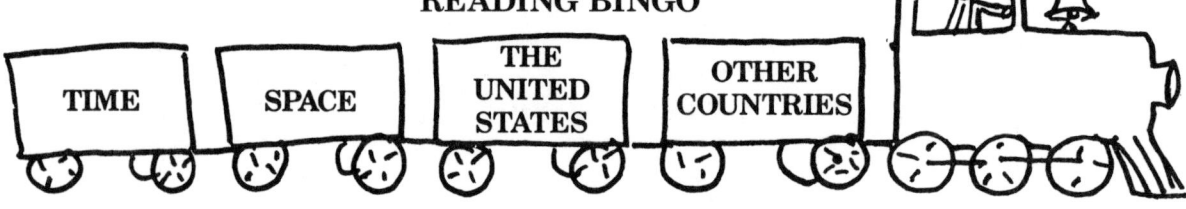

THE PAST FICTION	THE FUTURE FICTION	YOUR STATE NON-FICTION	ANOTHER COUNTRY FICTION	SPACE TRAVEL NON-FICTION
A STATE IN THE UNITED STATES NONFICTION	THE PAST NON-FICTION	ANOTHER COUNTRY NON-FICTION	A STATE IN THE UNITED STATES FICTION	SPACE TRAVEL FICTION
SPACE TRAVEL NON-FICTION	THE PAST FICTION	ANOTHER COUNTRY FICTION	A STATE IN THE UNITED STATES NON-FICTION	ANOTHER COUNTRY NON-FICTION
ANOTHER COUNTRY FICTION	YOUR STATE NON-FICTION	SPACE TRAVEL FICTION	SPACE TRAVEL NON-FICTION	THE FUTURE FICTION
THE FUTURE FICTION	SPACE TRAVEL NON-FICTION	THE PAST NON-FICTION	THE PAST FICTION	A STATE IN THE UNITED STATES FICTION

Record the titles of the books you have read in the appropriate square or on the back of this page.

Name _____ **Grade** _____

© 1989 by The Center for Applied Research in Education

Another Country

Fiction

Another Country

Non-Fiction

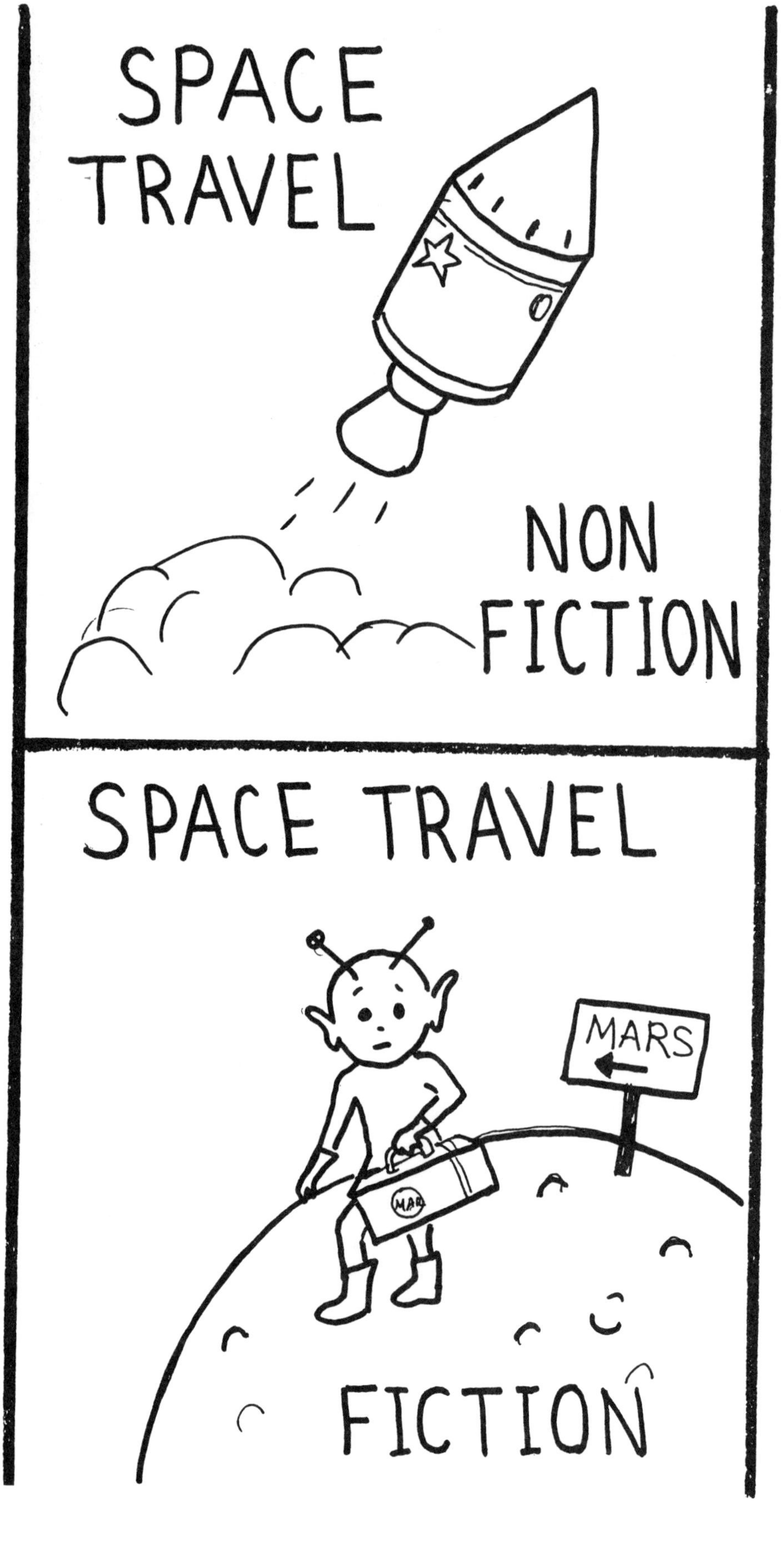
SPACE TRAVEL
NON FICTION
SPACE TRAVEL
MARS
FICTION

A STATE IN THE U.S.A.

NON-FICTION

A STATE IN THE U.S.A.

FICTION

YOUR STATE

NON-FICTION

THE FUTURE

FICTION

THE PAST – FICTION

THE PAST

NON-FICTION

LET'S TRAVEL WITH BOOKS!

BOOKS LET US TRAVEL!

TAKE TO THE SEAS IN BOOKS

VACATION TRAVEL TIME!
DON'T FORGET TO READ!

NOTE FROM HOME

_____
(Child's Name)

HAS READ THE BOOK:

_____

FOR THE LET'S TRAVEL READING BINGO!

....
(SIGNATURE OF PARENT OR ANOTHER RESPONSIBLE ADULT)

NOTE FROM HOME

_____
(Child's Name)

HAS READ THE BOOK:

_____

FOR THE LET'S TRAVEL READING BINGO!

....
(SIGNATURE OF PARENT OR ANOTHER RESPONSIBLE ADULT)

© 1989 by The Center for Applied Research in Education

THIS CERTIFIES THAT

HAS COMPLETED A BINGO IN THE

Let's Travel Reading Bingo

Signature of teacher or librarian

© 1989 by The Center for Applied Research in Education

B. Animal Reading Program for the Primary Grades

Teacher Directions

GRADE LEVELS: Kindergarten–Grade 3

While some second and third graders may be able to participate in the reading bingos there are few, if any, kindergarten or first grade students who could. This animal reading bingo gives kindergarten and first grade students as well as second and third graders the opportunity to do a reading activity. It is one they really enjoy.
DIRECTIONS: Print copies of the student record sheets. You will need quite a few, for most students will at least begin the reading activity. Make many copies of the animals on colored construction paper. You may want to first copy the sheets on white and cut them out so that you can reassemble them making a separate sheet with four or five cats on it and a separate one with four elephants on it since you will find that the students will read many more books about pets and wild animals than they do the other animals. If it is possible, get parent or older student volunteers to cut out the colored animals and put them in separate marked envelopes so that they will be readily accessible. Arrange for volunteer parents or very able older students to be in the library before school for the time of the reading program. These volunteers can help record the students' reading and hand out the appropriate animals. (You can also arrange to have each teacher do the recording, but the students do enjoy coming to the library for their animals and the teachers appreciate not having to do one more thing.)

This reading program is best done in April in connection with National Library Week and at a time when the older students are doing an "I LOVE BOOKS READING BINGO." It can be used at other times of the year but by spring many first graders can read well enough that they can participate. Kindergarten students can participate by allowing them to count books read to them by an adult.

Introduce the activity to the various classes by displaying several of the many different animal books available for them to read. Explain that they will get a prize if they read ten (or whatever number you think is suitable) animal books. For each animal book they read they will get a construction paper cut-out animal on which to write their name and the title of the book read. The kind of animal they receive will depend on the type of animal in the book which they have read. For example: if they read a book about any kind of wild animal—lion, tiger, squirrel, raccoon, etc., they

B. Animal Reading Program for the Primary Grades

will receive an elephant. If they read about any kind of a bird or fowl they receive a duck. For an amphibian or reptile they receive a turtle. For pets, dogs, rabbits, cats, etc., they receive a cut-out cat. For any water animal they receive a fish, and for any insect, spider, or things that crawl (caterpillars, worms, etc.) they receive a butterfly. These are to be filled in and then taken to their classroom. Each class may want to mount them in the hall beside their room.

If the recording is done in the library, have the record sheets for each classroom in separate folders so they may be found quickly. When the students bring in their filled-out note from home, record the title of the book, etc. on the record sheet and give the child the construction paper animal. Students in grades 2 and 3 could fill out the title and their name on the animal themselves, but for students in kindergarten and first grade the title may have to be filled in by you or a volunteer. The animals are then taken back to the classroom by the student so that they may be mounted in the hall. If you have room in the library they could also be mounted in the library, but most students enjoy seeing the growing parade of animals by their classroom door.

Prizes are not really necessary since the children do receive the construction paper animals, but prizes are nice to award if your library or school can afford it. Sometimes parent groups like the P.T.A. will fund the program, especially when they see how it encourages the younger children to read. Anything which is appropriate to an animal reading program is acceptable. Some ideas for prizes are: animal erasers or pencil tops, animal color or story books, tiny stuffed animals such as those with velcro which cling to pencils, an animal movie for the winners or for the classroom that reads the most books, a visit to a veterinarian or pet store or zoo, or a day when an employee from a zoo or pet shop could come to talk to the students and perhaps bring an animal for them to see. An added treat at either the beginning or end of the reading time would be to have a pet day where children bring their pets, or a stuffed pet day when students bring their favorite stuffed pet. The younger students may want to display or have a parade for the older students who aren't participating.

Note: Some students will read many more books than the number needed to win a prize, or the number on the record sheet. If they do, turn over the record sheet and record their books there since you don't want to limit the children in how much they can read.

NOTES:_____

_____

_____

_____

ANIMAL READING BOOKS RECORD SHEET FOR:

Name _____ Grade _____

TITLE OF BOOK	ANIMAL TYPE	DATE READ
1. _____	_____	_____
2. _____	_____	_____
3. _____	_____	_____
4. _____	_____	_____
5. _____	_____	_____
6. _____	_____	_____
7. _____	_____	_____
8. _____	_____	_____
9. _____	_____	_____
10. _____	_____	_____
11. _____	_____	_____
12. _____	_____	_____

HAPPY READING!

© 1989 by The Center for Applied Research in Education

BIRDS

TITLE

NAME

GRADE

TITLE

NAME

GRADE

WILD ANIMALS

TITLE

NAME

GRADE

AMPHIBIANS AND REPTILES

© 1989 by The Center for Applied Research in Education

TITLE

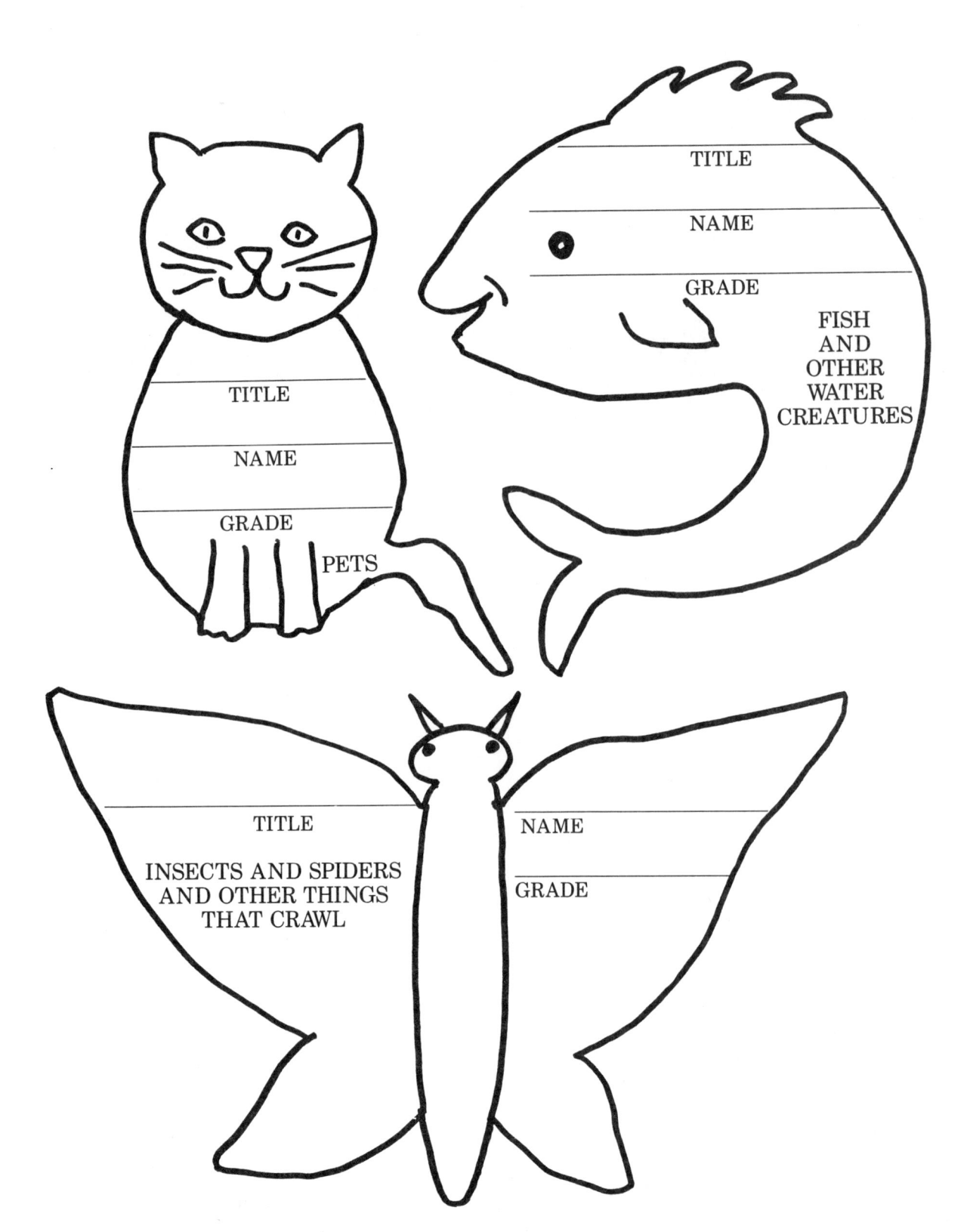

NAME

GRADE

FISH
AND
OTHER
WATER
CREATURES

TITLE

NAME

GRADE

PETS

TITLE

INSECTS AND SPIDERS
AND OTHER THINGS
THAT CRAWL

NAME

GRADE

© 1989 by The Center for Applied Research in Education

has read the book:	has read the book:
DATE:	DATE:
PARENT'S SIGNATURE	PARENT'S SIGNATURE
has read the book:	has read the book:
DATE:	DATE:
PARENT'S SIGNATURE	PARENT'S SIGNATURE

CONGRATULATIONS TO

_____

WHO HAS _____ BOOKS IN THE ANIMAL READING PROGRAM.

_____
LIBRARIAN'S SIGNATURE

_____
DATE

CONGRATULATIONS TO

_____

WHO HAS READ _____ BOOKS IN THE ANIMAL READING PROGRAM.

_____
LIBRARIAN'S SIGNATURE

_____
DATE

© 1989 by The Center for Applied Research in Education

C. Spring Student Detective Activities

**TEACHER'S PAGE FOR
"THE STUDENT DETECTIVE AND THE CASE OF THE APRIL FOOL
JOKER"**

GRADE LEVELS: 4–8
SKILLS USED: Research in almanac, a book of quotations, encyclopedia, *Famous First Facts*, and *The Guinness Book of World Records*

This Student Detective activity is difficult since it uses many different reference sources. Advanced or talented classes in grades 4–8 can probably do the work on their own as can most seventh and eighth grade classes. For less able or younger groups you will need to go through the clues to determine the reference source which is needed. Have them write beside each clue the reference book which they will need.

If you prefer, the activity can be used as a challenge or a contest or an extra credit activity. Another challenge or extra credit activity could be to have students write a new Student Detective case of their own.

KEY: 1. Audrey   2. Watson   3. ten   4. Harry

5. Roosevelt   6. Gordon   7. Stafford   8. four

Note: Clues 1, 3, 7, and 8 can be found in an almanac. Clue 2 in a book of quotations, *Bartlett's Familiar Quotations*, Clue 4 is found in *Famous First Facts*, and Clues 5 and 6 are answered in *The Guinness Book of World Records*.

NOTES:

THE STUDENT DETECTIVE
AND
THE CASE OF THE APRIL FOOL JOKER

Every classroom had been visited by an April Fool joker. Miss Bennett's lunch tickets were found in Mr. Garrett's room with a note saying only, "April Fool!"

Mrs. Abbott's blackboard had "April Fool" written all over it in colored chalk. The P. E. teacher found the basketballs where the baseball bats belong and the baseballs in the basketball cupboard along with a note saying, "April Fool!"

Finally the principal asked the Student Detective to find the April Fool joker. The Student Detective used her eyes, her ears, and her mind and she found the April Fool Joker. The Student Detective thinks that you, too, can figure out who the joker is if you follow the clues and use your reference skills to follow them.

CLUE #1: The Student Detective discovered that the joker was in the classroom of the teacher whose first name is the same as the first name of the actress who won the Academy Award for best actress in 1953.

CLUE #2: The teacher's last name is the same as the last name of the person who said, "April, April, Laugh thy girlish laughter. Then, the moment after, Weep thy girlish tears."

CLUE #3: The Student Detective found out that the April Fool Joker had played as many April Fool tricks as there are number of provinces in Canada.

CLUE #4: The Student Detective found out that the best friend of the joker had the same first name as the person who first invented the automobile tire chain.

CLUE #5: The friend's last name is the same as the last name of the person who holds the record for handshaking (as of 1985).

CLUE #6: The Student Detective followed the friend to the home of the joker who was seen writing "April Fool" notes. The joker's first name is the same as the first name of the man who was the world's richest man (as of 1985).

CLUE #7: His last name is the same as the last name of the person who won the Pulitzer Prize for fiction in 1970.

CLUE #8: The prankster admitted he had played the April Fool jokes and the principal told him to spend as many hours helping the teachers he had tricked as there were eclipses of the sun and moon in 1986.

YOUR ANSWERS:

The Student Detective found that the April Fool Joker was in the classroom of _____
1.
_____. The Joker had played _____ April Fool tricks. The best friend of the Joker was
2.   3.
_____ _____. The April Fool Joker was _____ _____.
4.   5.   6.   7.

The teacher made the Joker work _____ hours for playing jokes.
                                  8.

Name_____ Grade_____

© 1989 by The Center for Applied Research in Education

_____

is awarded the title of:

Super Student Detective

for solving the case of

The April Fool Joker

_____
Signature of teacher or librarian

_____ (date)

_____

is awarded the title of:

Super Student Detective

for solving the case of

The April Fool Joker

_____
Signature of teacher or librarian

_____ (date)

© 1989 by The Center for Applied Research in Education

TEACHER'S PAGE FOR "THE STUDENT DETECTIVE AND THE CASE OF THE MYSTERY INVITATION"

GRADE LEVELS: 5–8 (some fourth graders can do this activity)
SKILLS USED: Research in an encyclopedia, almanac, and dictionary

This activity is much easier than the preceding one and could probably be done by most fourth grade classes. Students in grades five through eight should be able to determine for themselves which reference source is needed to find the answer to each clue.

As an introduction to the activity you might show some Sherlock Holmes books or show a short film or sound filmstrip of one of the Sherlock Holmes books. Read the directions together and then let the students do the work independently. If you feel there may be some congestion in the reference section you could have students begin on different clues. Since many questions are answered in the almanac or dictionary this may not be necessary since most libraries have an adequate supply of these two reference books.

If the activity is done as a contest, challenge, or for extra credit it would be fun to take a picture of all the students who complete the activity correctly. Post the picture with a caption such as _____ School Famous Research Detectives. Their prize could be a Sherlock Holmes movie or another detective movie for children.

KEY: 1. 1859   2. Hughes   3. 22nd   4. three   5. five

6. soup   7. creole rice dish   8. pastry dessert

9. costume   10. good-natured joking

NOTE: Clues 1 and 3 are found in an encyclopedia. 2, 4, and 5 are found most easily in an almanac. 6, 7, 8, 9, and 10 are found in a dictionary or thesaurus.

THE STUDENT DETECTIVE AND THE CASE OF THE MYSTERY INVITATION

One beautiful day in May, the Student Detective was glancing through an almanac when he jumped up excitedly and yelled to his friend, Buzz, "Hey, Sir Conan Doyle, the author of the Sherlock Holmes books, was born in May! Sherlock Holmes is the greatest! Let's have a birthday party for the author! We'll invite anyone who can be a 'Sherlock Holmes' and figure out our invitations."

So the Student Detective and Buzz figured out their invitations and gave one to all the kids in their classroom. The invitations said, "All detectives who can figure out the clues below are invited to a party in honor of Sir Conan Doyle, author of the Sherlock Holmes books!"

COULD YOU HAVE GONE TO THIS PARTY? See if you can figure out the clues and put your answers in the spaces below.

CLUE #1: The house number where the party is to be is the same as the year when Sir Conan Doyle was born.

CLUE #2: The street where the house is located has the same name as the last name of the Pulitzer Prize winner for International Reporting in 1967.

CLUE #3: The party will be on the same date in May when Sir Conan Doyle was born.

CLUE #4: The party will begin at the same time in the afternoon as the number of counties in Delaware.

CLUE #5: The party will end at the same time as the number of counties in Rhode Island.

CLUE #'s 6 & 7: Hot *potage* will be served along with *jambalaya*.

CLUE #8: *Baklava* will also be served.

CLUE #9: Please come to the party as a *mummer* would.

CLUE #10: Be ready for a lot of *badinage* at the party.

YOUR ANSWERS:

Please come to a birthday party in honor of Sir Conan Doyle, author of the Sherlock Holmes books. The party will be at _____ South _____ Street on
                                              1.   2.

May _____. The party will begin at _____ and it will end at
        3.   4.

_____. We will serve _____ and _____. We will also serve
  5.   6.   7.

_____. Come to the party dressed in a _____. There will be a lot of
  8.   9.

_____ at the party. Please come.
  10.

Name _____ Grade _____

_____
is awarded the title of:

Super Student Detective

for solving

The Mystery Invitation

_____
Signature of teacher or librarian

_____
(Date)

© 1989 by The Center for Applied Research in Education

_____
is awarded the title of:

Super Student Detective

for solving

The Mystery Invitation

_____
Signature of teacher or librarian

_____
(Date)

D. Spring Crossword Count Puzzles

TEACHER'S PAGE FOR "SPRING CROSSWORD COUNT PUZZLES"

GRADE LEVELS: All grade levels from 1–Adult

If you have not previously used the Crossword Count Puzzles, please see the directions in the first unit—AUTUMN CROSSWORD COUNT PUZZLES.

RECORD OF SCORES FOR SPRINGTIME CROSSWORD COUNT PUZZLES

RECORD OF SCORES FOR "WELCOME SPRING CROSSWORD COUNT"			
YEAR	GRADE	SCORE	PERSON ACHIEVING THE SCORE

(Continued on next page)

RECORD OF SCORES FOR A BUSY TIME FOR BEES CROSSWORD COUNT			

Additional Crossword Count Puzzles can be obtained from QUAILRIDGE MEDIA, Selma Oregon

WELCOME SPRING
CROSSWORD COUNT

FIND THREE WORDS TO FIT IN THIS CROSSWORD COUNT PUZZLE FOR SPRING. USE THE DICTIONARY TO FIND WORDS WITH HIGH POINT LETTERS. *REMEMBER*: A WORD MAY BE USED ONLY ONCE AND YOU MAY NOT USE PROPER NOUNS IN THIS PUZZLE. GOOD LUCK!

LETTER POINT COUNT

A: 14	N: 22
B: 10	O: 20
C: 11	P: 25
D: 19	Q: 2
E: 15	R: 24
F: 1	S: 26
G: 21	T: 16
H: 3	U: 13
I: 23	V: 6
J: 4	W: 17
K: 12	X: 5
L: 18	Y: 8
M: 9	Z: 7

Crossword grid with SPRING across the top, and numbered boxes 1-14 around the border.

© 1989 by The Center for Applied Research in Education

YOUR POINT COUNT:

Box 1: _____ Box 2: _____ Box 3: _____ Box 4: _____ Box 5: _____ Box 6: _____

Box 7: _____ Box 8: _____ Box 9: _____ Box 10: _____ Box 11: _____ Box 12: _____

Box 13: _____ Box 14: _____

MY TOTAL SCORE IS: _____

Name _____ **Grade** _____

1st

_____

HAS WON FIRST PLACE IN THE

Welcome Spring

CROSSWORD COUNT CONTEST.

_____

TEACHER/LIBRARIAN

DATE:_____

2nd

_____

HAS WON SECOND PRIZE IN THE

Welcome Spring

CROSSWORD COUNT CONTEST.

_____

TEACHER/LIBRARIAN

DATE:_____

© 1989 by The Center for Applied Research in Education

A BUSY TIME FOR BEES!

CROSSWORD COUNT

Be busy as bees while you use the dictionary to see how many points you can get in this BUSY BEES CROSSWORD COUNT PUZZLE. Remember that words must not be proper nouns.
  GOOD LUCK!

A: 13
B: 12
C: 11
D: 10
E: 23
F: 0
G: 8
H: 26
I: 7
J: 4
K: 5
L: 21
M: 2
N: 24
O: 25
P: 20
Q: 8
R: 14
S: 15
T: 16
U: 17
V: 18
W: 19
X: 1
Y: 22
Z: 3

YOUR SCORE:

Box 1: _____   Box 2: _____   Box 3: _____

Box 4: _____   Box 5: _____   Box 6: _____

Box 7: _____   Box 8: _____   Box 9: _____

Box 10: _____   Box 11: _____

MY TOTAL SCORE IS: _____

Name_____   Grade_____

© 1989 by The Center for Applied Research in Education

_____

HAS WON FIRST PLACE IN THE

Busy Time for Bees

CROSSWORD COUNT CONTEST.

_____
TEACHER/LIBRARIAN

DATE:_____

_____

HAS WON SECOND PRIZE IN THE

Busy Time for Bees

CROSSWORD COUNT CONTEST.

_____
TEACHER/LIBRARIAN

DATE:_____

E. Research Activities for Spring

**TEACHER'S PAGE FOR
"SPRINGTIME IS BIRD TIME"**

GRADE LEVELS: 4–6
SKILLS USED: Research in almanac or encyclopedia, and use of card catalog.

Since students must use both the almanac and the card catalog for this activity, congestion at the card catalog can be avoided by starting four people (one for each question of part 2) at the card catalog. Let the rest of the class use the almanac and then go to the card catalog as they finish since most will not finish at the same time. An extra activity could be for students to draw the state bird of their state on the back of the activity sheet.

Another optional activity could be for students to see how many fiction books they could find which contain a bird or a type of bird in the title.

KEY: 1. North Carolina: Cardinal 2. New Mexico: roadrunner
3. Maine: chickadee 4. Mississippi: mockingbird
5. New Hampshire: purple finch 6. Michigan: robin
7. Alabama: yellowhammer 8. Utah: seagull
9. Georgia: brown thrasher 10. New York: bluebird

A. Dewey Decimal Number for birds is 598.2
B. Answers will vary according to your collection.
C. Answers will vary.
D. Answers will vary.

NOTES:_____
_____
_____
_____

SPRINGTIME IS BIRD TIME!

After a long winter many birds return to sing their songs and build their nests.

Each state in the United States chooses a bird to be their state bird. Find the state bird for each state below.

1. North Carolina: _____

2. New Mexico: _____

3. Maine: _____

4. Mississippi: _____

5. New Hampshire: _____

6. Michigan: _____

7. Alabama: _____

8. Utah: _____

9. Georgia: _____

10. New York: _____

USE THE CARD CATALOG TO ANSWER THE FOLLOWING QUESTIONS.

A. What is the Dewey Decimal number for birds? _____

B. Write the title and author of a book which your library has about eagles. _____

C. Write the title and author of a book which your library has about penguins. _____

D. Write the title and author of a book which your library has about owls. _____

Describe your state bird. _____

_____

_____

_____

_____

_____

Name_____   Grade_____

© 1989 by The Center for Applied Research in Education

E. Research Activities for Spring

TEACHER'S PAGE FOR "HELP THE BUNNY FIND HIS BASKET!"

GRADE LEVELS: 4–8
SKILLS USED: Research in almanac, card catalog, and dictionary.

By this time of the year students in grades 5 through 8 should need little help with the activity. Students in grade 4 may need help in finding and using the perpetual calendar and with using the temperature and precipitation charts.

The activity begins with two questions in the almanac which should help overcrowding at any one reference section since most school libraries have enough almanacs and dictionaries for most groups. If you feel there may be crowding at the card catalog have one child begin on question 3 and another on question 5, or start other students on all the questions so that they will be needing to use the card catalog at different times.

An extra activity could be for students to write their own questions for the bunny. Make a copy of this activity and cut out the question section. Then make copies of it so that students can be given the sheet with the question section blank. Let them write their own questions for others in the class to answer.

KEY: 1. Monday   2. May 14th   3. Answers will vary depending upon your library's collection   4. Answers will vary depending on the dictionary used   5. Irene Hunt   6. Tupelo, Mississippi   7. 70 degrees (answers could vary if figures in almanac change in different years)   8. 5.4 inches (answers could vary depending upon year of the almanac)   9. Feeling of happiness or excited cheerfulness

NOTES:

HELP THE BUNNY FIND HIS BASKET!

This bunny has lost his basket. Help him by answering each question on the left. Put your answers on the path which the bunny must take to find the basket.

1. On what day of the week will April Fool's day fall in the year 2002?
2. Mother's Day is the 2nd Sunday in May. What will be the date of Mother's Day in the year 2000?
3. Look in the card catalog and find a book about rabbits. Write the title and author of that book in the blank for number 3.
4. What are the dictionary guide words on the page where the word rabbit is found?
5. Who wrote *Across Five Aprils*?
6. This rabbit is afraid of tornadoes in the spring. Where was there a tornado on April 5, 1936?
7. Some states are very warm in April. What is the average normal temperature for April in San Antonio, Texas?
8. Some states have a lot of rain in April. What is the average rainfall for Mobile, Alabama in April?
9. Spring makes us feel "euphoric." What does this mean?

1. _____
2. _____
3. Title: _____
   author _____
4. _____ and _____
5. _____
6. _____
7. _____
8. _____
9. _____

Name _____ Grade _____

© 1989 by The Center for Applied Research in Education

E. Research Activities for Spring

TEACHER'S PAGE FOR
"DICTIONARY FUN FOR MOTHER'S DAY"

GRADE LEVELS: 2–4
SKILLS USED: Dictionary research

This activity gives more practice in using the dictionary. Since there are only six words to look up, most students should be able to do the activity during the class time.

Give each student a dictionary. Go over the directions with the class. Provide crayons if some students wish to color the pictures they draw in the box.

An extra activity for students who finish early or for another class session, could be for the students to use the dictionary to see if they can find a gift suitable for Mother for each letter of the alphabet. Tell them they must be able to describe each gift, if they put down a word for which they do not know the meaning.

KEY:
1. victuals—food
2. confectioneries—candies
3. chapeau—hat or bonnet
4. bumbershoot—umbrella
5. valise—suitcase
6. calendulas—orange and yellow flowers

NOTES:_____

DICTIONARY FUN FOR MOTHER'S DAY!

Look up the underlined words in each square in a dictionary. Then follow the directions. Write the dictionary guide words for each word you find in the blanks at the top of each box.

_____ _____ | _____ _____

Mothers are good at making *victuals*. Make some victuals for Mother in this box. | Some people give their mother *confectioneries* for Mother's Day. Make some confectioneries in the box above.

_____ _____ | _____ _____

Mothers look pretty in a new *chapeau*. Draw a mother in a new chapeau. | A new *bumbershoot* might be a nice gift for Mother on Mother's Day. Draw one in the box above.

_____ _____ | _____ _____

Do you think your mother might like a new *valise* for Mother's Day. Draw one above. | Some *calendulas* would make a nice gift for Mother on Mother's Day. Draw some above.

Name_____ **Grade**_____

E. Research Activities for Spring

TEACHER'S PAGE FOR
"IT HAPPENED IN THE SPRINGTIME"

GRADE LEVELS: 4–8
SKILLS USED: Research in the almanac and thinking skills

This activity involves finding answers in the almanac and then crossing those answers off on the grid. The remaining letters in the grid form a message.

By this time of year most fourth graders as well as the older students can do this activity independently. The answers can all be found in alamancs dated after 1978. Most schools have enough almanacs so that each child may have an almanac to use. If not, have the students work in pairs.

Advanced or gifted groups could be encouraged at another class session to write their own secret message using research questions. If they do, encourage them by copying their activity and letting the students try to discover the message.

KEY: 1. Wednesday   2. Italy   3. Lemon   4. Baltimore
   5. bluegrass   6. Nebraska   7. Arkansas
   8. Magnolia   9. Mitchell   10. Grant

The Secret message is: You are an almanac expert. Now you can quickly find out many things.

NOTES:

1.
2.
3.
4.
5.
6.
7.
8.
9.
10.

IT HAPPENED IN THE SPRINGTIME

USE YOUR RESEARCH SKILLS AND THE ALMANAC TO ANSWER THE FOLLOWING QUESTIONS. THEN CROSS OFF YOUR ANSWERS IN THE GRID BELOW. (THE REMAINING LETTERS WILL SPELL A MESSAGE!) (A blacked-in square means a period in the message.)

1. Flag Day is cleebrated on June 14th. Use the perpetual calendar to find out on what day of the week it will be celebrated in the year 2000. _____
2. Earthquakes sometime occur in the spring. In what country was there a major earthquake on May 6, 1976? _____
3. The Academy Awards for excellence in Motion Picutres are awarded in the spring. Who won the Academy Award for best actor in 1973? (Last name only.) _____
4. The NBA (National Basketball Association) has its championship playoffs in the spring. Who won the championship in 1948? _____
5. Kentucky became a state on June 1, 1972. What is this state's nickname? _____ State
6. Arbor Day is celebrated in most states in April. Where was this holiday first celebrated? _____
7. What state was first admitted to the Union on June 15, 1836? _____
8. Louisiana became a state on April 30, 1812. What is the state flower of Louisiana? _____
9. The Pulitzer Prizes are awarded in the spring of each year. What is the last name of the winner of the Pulitzer Prize for Fiction in 1937? _____
10. Our 18th President was born on April 27th. What is his last name? _____

NOW CROSS OFF YOUR ANSWERS FROM ABOVE ON THE GRID BELOW. THEN USE THE REMAINING LETTERS TO FORM A MESSAGE.

1.	Y	W	O	E	D	N	U	E	S	D	A	A	Y
2.	R	E	I	A	T	N	A	A	L	L	M	Y	A
3.	N	L	A	E	C	M	E	M	X	P	O	E	N
4.	R	B	A	T	L	T	I	■	M	O	N	R	E
5.	B	O	L	U	W	E	G	R	Y	A	S	O	S
6.	N	U	E	C	B	A	R	N	A	Q	S	K	A
7.	U	A	R	I	K	A	C	N	K	S	A	L	S
8.	Y	M	A	F	I	G	N	O	N	L	D	I	A
9.	O	M	I	U	T	C	H	M	E	A	L	L
10.	N	G	Y	T	H	R	I	N	G	S	A	N	T

AND THE MESSAGE IS: _____

Name_____ Grade_____

© 1989 by The Center for Applied Research in Education

E. Research Activities for Spring

TEACHER'S PAGE FOR
"A SUMMER VACATION IN CANADA"

GRADE LEVELS: 4–8

This activity requires research in the encyclopedia, almanac, and the *Guinness Book of Records*. Since these references are not difficult some fourth graders and most fifth through eighth graders should be able to do the activity independently. Others may need help in identifying the reference book needed to answer the questions.

Read the directions together in class and discuss if there are any questions. If necessary do the first questions so that students can see that the letter in the box should be placed in the first space in the sentence at the bottom of the page. If limited reference materials are a problem, assign each student or several students to begin on different questions. Since many questions can be answered by using the almanac and most schools have an adequate supply of almanacs, there may not be a problem with adequate reference materials.

ADDITIONAL ACTIVITIES: In a subsequent class or for advanced students have the students prepare a similar activity to this one, except they could use interesting vacation places in their own state or in the United States in place of the Canadian ones used in the activity. Students could work on their activity sheets in three- or four-member teams and when the activities are completed the teams could exchange their activity sheets and do the work required for the other team's paper. Advanced groups or those groups that enjoy a contest could see which team can complete the other team's paper first.

> KEY: 1. Victoria   2. Newfoundland   3. Alberta
> 4. Vancouver   5. Edmonton   6. Toronto
> 7. Wood Buffalo National Park (*1986 Guinness Book of Records*)
> 8. Ontario   9. Charlottetown   10. Quebec

NOTES:

A SUMMER VACATION IN CANADA

Canada, the largest country in the northern hemisphere, is a favorite place to visit for many people in the United States. Here are some families who plan to visit Canada this summer. See if you can use research skills to find out where they plan to visit.

1. The Brownings plan to visit the beautiful Butchart Gardens which are in __ __ __ __ __ __ ☐, the capital of the province of British Columbia.
2. The Faber family plans to visit the city of St. John's which is the capital of __ __ __ __ __ ☐ __ __ __ __ __ __.
3. Erin and Dustin and their family plan to visit Lake Louise which is in the province of __ __ __ __ __ ☐ __.
4. Jeff, Jeremy, and Nikki hope their parents will take them to beautiful Stanley Park in the city of __ __ __ __ ☐ __ __ __ __.
5. Jan and Levi and their family plan to visit __ __ ☐ __ __ __ __ __, which is the capital of Alberta.
6. Dan and Bob hope to visit __ ☐ __ __ __ __ __ , the home of the Maple Leafs Hockey Team.
7. When Lori and Eden and their family go to Canada they hope to visit __ __ __ ☐ __ __ __ __ __ __ National Park, which is the largest park in the world.
8. Larry's family plan to visit the Canadian province which has the biggest population of any province. That province is __ __ __ __ __ ☐ __.
9. Josh and Michael's family is traveling to __ __ __ ☐ __ __ __ __ __ __ __, the capital of Prince Edward Island province.
10. Jessica's family plans to visit the largest province in Canada, which is __ __ ☐ __ __ __ __.

If you answered the above questions correctly, you can find out how all of these families traveled in Canada. Take the letter you put in each box and write them in the blanks below.

All of the families traveled by __ __ __ __ __ __ __ __ __ __ __.

Name_____ Grade_____

© 1989 by The Center for Applied Research in Education

E. Research Activities for Spring

TEACHER'S PAGE FOR
"HIP, HIP, HOORAY FOR FATHER'S DAY"

GRADE LEVELS: 4–6

Father's Day can provide an opportunity for students to practice finding Dewey Decimal numbers in the non-fiction section of the library.

HIP, HIP, HOORAY FOR FATHER'S DAY provides this practice and it also requires that students do a little thinking to decide on the right answer. When explaining the activity to them tell them that when they find the right Dewey Decimal number on the call number of a book, they should examine several books with that number and then decide on the most logical answer that fits the sentence.

This page also has a section in which students use the card catalog to find authors and call numbers of books with "Father" in the title. To prevent congestion at the card catalog, it is a good idea to start three of the students at the card catalog, and the others can do this section when they complete the ten Dewey Decimal blanks.

An extra activity might be a scavenger hunt by letting students go in groups of two and see which pair can find the most books with members of the family in the title; i.e., "mother," "sister," "brother," "father," "grandmother," etc. Another activity would be to have children look in the non-fiction section to find a book which their father might like. Have them show the book and explain why it is appropriate for their father.

KEY: 1. dog or puppy   2. poetry   3. dinosaur (your library may have dinosaur books under "560"—if so, tell the children to change the number)   4. plants (flowers, trees, etc. would be acceptable)   5. atlas   6. football   7. airplane   8. cooking   9. jokes and riddles   10. California

1. Beverly Cleary Fic, Cl   2. Peggy Mann Fic, Ma   3. Ruth Gannett Fic, Ga

HIP, HIP, HOORAY FOR FATHER'S DAY

On Father's Day, which is on the third Sunday in June, we like to show our fathers how much we think of them by giving them presents or by doing nice things for them. Use the Dewey Decimal numbers in the non-fiction section of the library to find out what the fathers below received from their children.

1. Jason and Joshua gave their father a tiny (636.7) _____ for Father's Day.
2. Jennifer gave her father a book of (808.1) _____ for Father's Day.
3. Jessica's father likes to build models so she gave him a model kit to build a (568) _____.
4. Brian's dad spends a lot of time in the backyard so Brian gave him a book about (581) _____.
5. Lisa's father likes to travel so Lisa gave him a (912) _____.
6. Dustin's dad likes sports so he gave him a book about (796.33) _____.
7. Erin gave her dad a battery-operated (629.13) _____.
8. Jeff gave his dad a book about (641) _____.
9. Jeremy's dad likes books that make him amused so Jeremy gave him a book of (808.7) _____.
10. Nikki gave her dad a book about his home state which is (979.4) _____.

NOW GO TO THE CARD CATALOG AND FIND THE AUTHOR AND THE CALL NUMBER OF THESE BOOKS WITH FATHER IN THE TITLE.

1. *Ramona and Her Father* by _____ Call Number: _____
2. *My Dad Lives in a Downtown Hotel* by _____ Call Number: _____
3. *My Father's Dragon* by _____ Call Number: _____

© 1989 by The Center for Applied Research in Education

Name_____ Grade_____

E. Research Activities for Spring

TEACHER'S PAGE FOR "THROUGH THE SUMMERTIME"

GRADE LEVELS: 4–6

Here is a quick and easy activity for one of the last weeks before summer vacation. Most of the answers in this activity can be found in the almanac or encyclopedia. Two answers are in a dictionary or thesaurus. By this time of year, even students in grade four will probably be able to do the work without help.

Some extra activities which might be used in conjunction with this activity could be to have each student write a research question about something he has done or will do during the summer or a question about a place he or she has visited, will visit, or would like to visit during the summer. These could be activities to do as the students complete the page or could be done during another class period. Another activity could be to ask the students to turn the paper over (when they have completed the work) and then scan the shelves for three or four books which they think they would like to read during the summer. They could write the titles and authors on the back of the activity page and each student could contribute his or her best title to a compiled list of "Favorite Books to Read for the Summer." This list could be typed and distributed to the class before summer begins.

KEY: 1. Chicago, Illinois   2. South Dakota   3. fireworks   4. swimming pool   5. Providence   6. Canada   7. Philadelphia, Pa.   8. Jackson, Mississippi

NOTES:

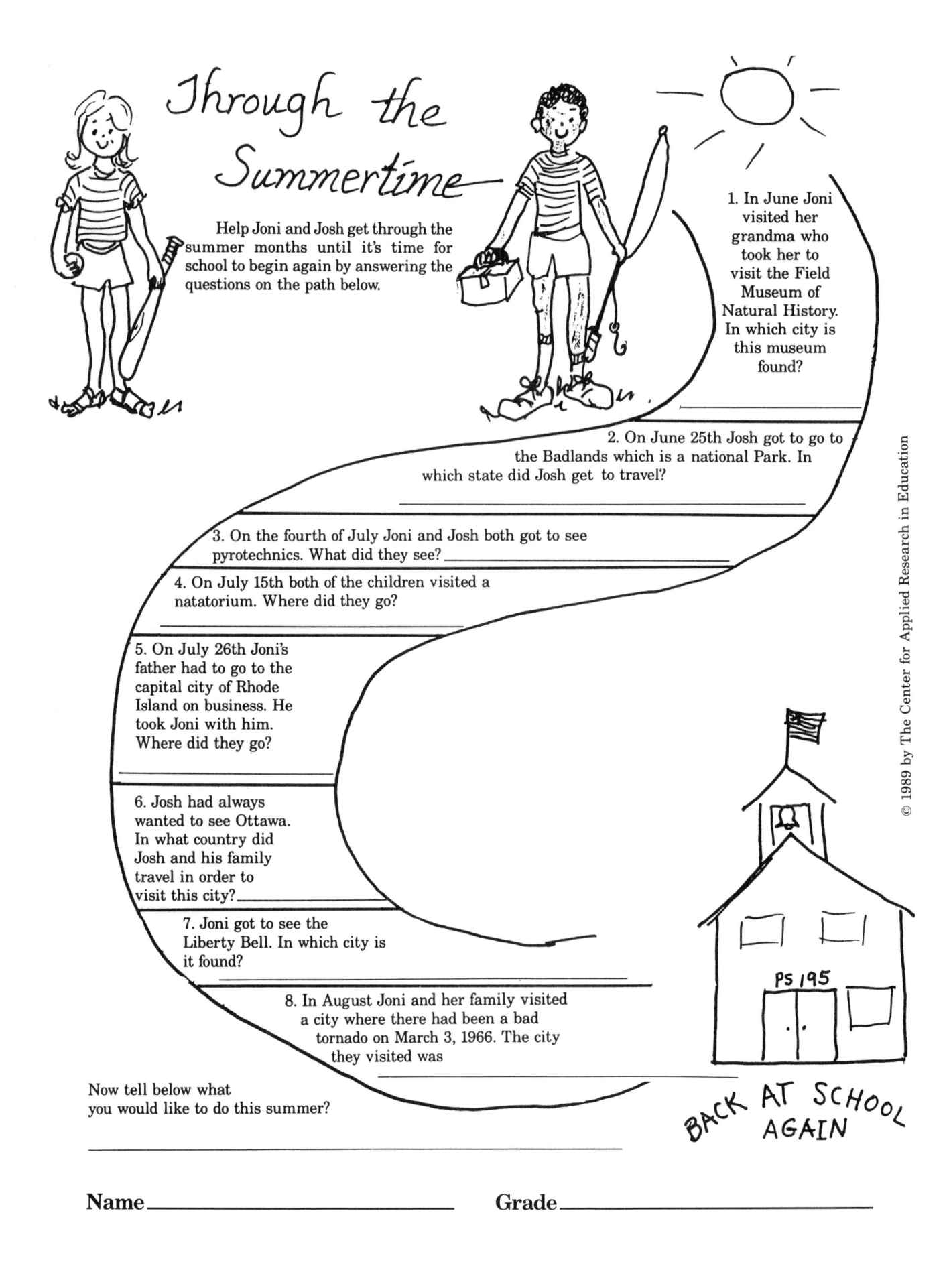

Through the Summertime

Help Joni and Josh get through the summer months until it's time for school to begin again by answering the questions on the path below.

1. In June Joni visited her grandma who took her to visit the Field Museum of Natural History. In which city is this museum found? _____

2. On June 25th Josh got to go to the Badlands which is a national Park. In which state did Josh get to travel? _____

3. On the fourth of July Joni and Josh both got to see pyrotechnics. What did they see? _____

4. On July 15th both of the children visited a natatorium. Where did they go? _____

5. On July 26th Joni's father had to go to the capital city of Rhode Island on business. He took Joni with him. Where did they go? _____

6. Josh had always wanted to see Ottawa. In what country did Josh and his family travel in order to visit this city? _____

7. Joni got to see the Liberty Bell. In which city is it found? _____

8. In August Joni and her family visited a city where there had been a bad tornado on March 3, 1966. The city they visited was _____

Now tell below what you would like to do this summer?
_____

BACK AT SCHOOL AGAIN

Name _____ Grade _____

© 1989 by The Center for Applied Research in Education